What Lurks Beyond

What Lurks Beyond

THE Paranormal IN Your Backyard

Jason Offutt

Truman State University Press

Cover: Dimitri Castrique Ploegsteert, "Final Destiny I: Lost in Ploegsteert's Woods."
Stock.xchng, no. 997469. Used by permission.

Cover design: Teresa Wheeler
Photos courtesy of the author unless otherwise noted.
Type: Minion Pro, Myriad Pro, and Sanvito © Adobe Systems Inc.
Printed by: Thomson-Shore, Dexter, Michigan USA

Library of Congress Cataloging-in-Publication Data

Offutt, Jason, 1965–
    What lurks beyond : The paranormal in your backyard / Jason Offutt.
        p. cm.
    ISBN 978-1-935503-03-3 (pbk. : alk. paper)
    1. Supernatural. 2. Middle West—Miscellanea. I. Title.
    BF1434.U6O38 2010
    130.977—dc22
                                                                    2009053255

Contents

Foreword

I have always held that there isn't a square millimeter on this planet that isn't haunted in some way. The memories, imprints, and life residues of every living thing throughout history has gone into the "blood and the bones" of Earth upon death, leaving behind psychic records we perceive as ghostly phenomena. We don't tune in to everything that has lived and died over millions of years, of course, which is a good thing, lest we feel squeezed right out of our space. But anywhere we go, we can find the phantom imprints of the past. We can also find openings or doorways into other dimensions, populated by odd beings, some of which we know as cryptids.

The mysterious, haunted, and bizarre are quite literally everywhere. In this enchanting collection of supernatural strangeness, Jason Offutt aptly demonstrates that you needn't look farther than your own backyard for amazing paranormal phenomena and experiences. The paranormal coexists with us all the time.

Offutt casts a 100-mile net from his home to demonstrate the variety of experiences awaiting the curious, and serves up a delicious menu of engaging firsthand accounts. Like me, you will keep turning the pages to see what he uncovers next. From my own experiences researching the paranormal for many years, I know, as does Offutt, that he has hit only the tip of things within his 100-mile radius. His point is that you don't have to look very far to have some rocking good paranormal adventures. Making pilgrimages to world-famous sites is fun, to be sure, but you can find equally exciting places right at your doorstep.

It is important for us, we the living, to get out there to explore what is "out there." Science makes only a half-hearted attempt to understand the paranormal. The fact is that most of what we know about the paranormal comes from our own subjective experiences. The paranormal is slippery with no clear boundaries, a shape-shifting entity in and of itself. We know what lies "out there" only through our own testimonies, corroborated by some hard evidence, historical data, and the testimonies of others.

By exploring the paranormal, we participate in an eternal record of everything that goes on in our little corner of the multiverse, part of the All That Is. We transcend time and space to touch a greater reality. Take a page from Jason's book—open your own back door and find out what lurks beyond!

—Rosemary Ellen Guiley

Acknowledgments

This is a big "thank you" to Nancy Rediger and Barbara Smith-Mandell at Truman State University Press for taking a chance on publishing my books on the paranormal. I would also like to thank Will Murphy and Brady Cummings for standing atop a lonely hill in a freezing Kansas cemetery, listening to the coyotes howl while we waited for something paranormal that never materialized. And I would also like to thank Northwest Missouri State University student Laura Boden (who has probably graduated by now) for her help in researching chapter 3: "Something Fell from the Sky: Skidmore, Missouri."

This is dedicated to them and to all of those people in this book who have encountered things that, frankly, give me the willies.

Introduction
Outside Your Back Door

What's outside your back door? No, seriously. What's out there? The lawn? Crickets? A tree or two? Neighbors? Or, depending on your part of the planet, tigers, baboons, entirely too much sand, or if you're lucky, billboards for chicken restaurants. The answer is everything is outside your back door. Let me repeat, everything. Everything you can imagine, and even things you can't imagine, exists on the other side of a thin glass pane and a mesh screen that is designed, and completely fails, to keep bugs out of your house. And although I usually score high on polls where the question is "Do you like to keep bugs out of your house," I still open the back door a lot. You know, just to see what's out there.

And when I started looking, I mean really looking—research, interviews, investigations—what I found was exciting, crazy, unbelievable, sometimes brown, enlightening, and quite definitely true. I was surrounded by the paranormal. Who'd a thunk it?

The paranormal, a topic formerly known as the supernatural, simply means "beyond normal." Ghosts, UFOs, cryptids (creatures unclassified by science), telepathy, demonology, anomalous structures on the moon and Mars, time travel, out-of-place artifacts, and many other topics qualify as paranormal simply because science hasn't given them a pat on the back and let them into the club. For the longest time, the giant panda and mountain gorilla were considered bunk. Now we look at them in zoos. According to biographer, essayist, and philosopher Elbert Hubbard (1856–1915), "The Supernatural is the Natural, just not yet understood." With *What Lurks Beyond*, I hope to offer a little understanding of the usually hidden world that surrounds us.

And what a world it is. Since humans developed culture and began writing down their religions, philosophies, dirty limericks, and the happenings of daily life, they included the paranormal—how *would* a Stone Age culture explain thunder anyway? Ghosts have been, and continue to be, present in every culture on the globe as are, to a lesser extent, demons, vampires, and werewolves. Ancient stories of lake monsters are common throughout the world, as are stories of large, hairy, manlike creatures that dwell in forests. In North America we call it Bigfoot or Sasquatch, in medieval Europe it was called the Wild Man of the Forest; Russia has the Almas, Tibet has the Yeti, and even Australia has its legends of these creatures known as the Yowie. Reports of unidentified objects flying in our skies and their inhabitants interacting with humans have existed for millennia. Like the Sumerian creation story where the Anunnaki—people from another planet in our solar system—came to Earth and created the human race by interbreeding with primitive man. The Dogon tribe of West Africa, which has existed since at least 3200 BC, believes it was visited by a race of beings that came to earth on an "ark" from a companion star to Sirius—even though that star is invisible without the use of a powerful telescope. In 1561, the skies over Nuremberg, Germany, were filled with flying spheres, cylinders, and crosses seemingly engaged in battle. And is the famous Schirmer UFO encounter in Ashland, Nebraska (detailed in chapter 28) explained by science? No. Is it fascinating? Yes.

The criteria for stories that appear in this book are: (1) the events had to be paranormal, and (2) they must have occurred within one hundred miles of my house (as the crow flies). Why? I wanted to prove that the paranormal is not just in remote mountains of the Pacific Northwest, the lochs of Scotland, in some secret lab in Roswell, New Mexico, or deep in the jungles of South America. No matter where you live on this planet, within a hundred miles of where you're sitting in your quiet, warm, comfortable chair, exist things that will make you scream for your mother. Some of the thirty-two stories in this book are long, others—just as serious, but not quite as complex—take many fewer words to tell, but they are all complete accounts of something a person encountered and could not explain—and these stories are real. I found people who have seen Bigfoot, have traveled in time, have been possessed by demons, are haunted by monsters, have encountered UFOs, have been terrified by black-eyed kids, or have seen things that are just generally weird ... and I didn't have to go far.

Over the past century or so there has been a rise of interest in all things paranormal, from the popularity of the Spiritualist movement of the late 1800s and early 1900s that advocated talking to the dead, to a resurgence in sightings of the Loch Ness monster started by the famous (or infamous) "Surgeon's Photograph" published in 1934; modern UFO encounters punctuated by the airship wave of 1897, the Foo Fighters of World War II, Roswell, and more recent sightings such as that in Stephenville, Texas; the alien abduction phenomena; and a greater interest in using modern technology to capture images and voices of ghosts. Some people are terrified of these topics, others (like me) are fascinated. The Internet has birthed a worldwide community of paranormal enthusiasts, taking over from the old media that had long since abandoned them. Ghosts and giants were treated as serious topics in the 1800s and a UFO sighting was a front-page story in the 1940s and 1950s. But during the Cold War, the subject of the paranormal was largely ignored by the mass media. It has only been since the end of the Cold War that paranormal topics have sprung back to life. Dr. Bryn Gribben, assistant professor of English at Northwest Missouri State University, said interest in the paranormal is a common reflection of society. "The twentieth century in England, they have an absence in ghosts [in literature] because they have so many things to worry about," she relates. "World War I, World War II, the end of the Empire. There's too much anxiety to deal with. It's almost like ghosts are leisure time." Today, although stresses abound, we Americans do like our leisure time. Let's take you, for example.

What's outside your back door? I'll tell you what's outside mine. I'm walking down the back steps. There it is—my back door. Pushing it open, I find a broken lawn mower, scattered toys, a dew-covered spider web, and tales of the paranormal. All are strange, close to home, and true—even the guy with the time machine. As British geneticist J. B. S. Haldane once said, "My own suspicion is that the Universe is not only queerer than we suppose, but queerer than we *can* suppose."

Where do *you* have to go to find stories of the fantastic? You have a back door, don't you? Open it.

1

They Call It David

Quiet hills roll just beyond the neighborhood where the Sherlock house sits, occasional trees dot the landscape once home to fields and prairie grass. The modest house was built in the mid-1970s on the outskirts of this small college town, home to Northwest Missouri State University (NWMSU) and boyhood home of motivational author and speaker Dale Carnegie. Save for his time in college and dental school, Gary Sherlock has lived in Maryville his entire life. When he was a child, there was no neighborhood on the land where he and his wife later bought their house and raised their family. Sherlock remembers, "When I was young I used to roam over here. This would have been in the '50s. It was all open ground then." Except for the barn. Sherlock remembers a barn sitting on the slope near the spot that would later be his house. Could the barn—or an accompanying house that fell long before Sherlock ran over these hills—have been the site of something horrific?

One of the Sherlocks' three daughters, Susan (Sherlock) McFee of Kansas City, wonders if it may have been. "My parents' house is haunted," McFee said, "and things started happening from the first day they moved in." The Sherlocks moved into the home with Susan, Lori, and Michelle in 1975 and soon realized they were not alone. "All my life I've heard voices whispering in the night," McFee said. "We've all heard that. You'll be the only one home and you'll hear the drawers squeaking away. Cabinets slamming. Doors slamming. I was a baby, I was one, but my mom tells the story—there was no way to get into the basement, and they heard people talking in the basement. And there was no one there." Lori (Sherlock) Durbin, still lives in Maryville and has taught in the communications department at the university for nineteen years. She remembers those early days in the house well: "Susan had a friend who said someone was sitting on the end of the bed and was bouncing up and down. She didn't know about the ghost, she just came up scared out of our basement." Although events such as disappearing silverware, frequently faulty appliances, and the sound of drawers opening and closing have happened throughout the house, "a lot of the encounters, at least early on, were in the basement," Durbin said, a place Sherlock admits "seems a lot colder sometimes than other times."

But the encounters soon left the basement and became more personal. "The cleaning lady quit because she said something attacked her," said McFee. That something, the cleaning lady told Sherlock, was a "little furry animal running around." Many people—except Sherlock—have seen a hairy creature skittering across the floor, but no one has ever been able to capture more than a glimpse of the creature. Not even enough to determine what kind of animal it is—or was. The thing ran into McFee when she was just a year old. "My mom said something knocked me over," she relates. "It was a brown furry thing. The cleaning lady said something cornered her and growled at her and it was gone. My parents have five cats. But it wasn't it." Nor was it their dog, who wags his tail for no apparent reason, then seems to react to something no one else can see.

The girls grew up, moved out of the Sherlock house, got married, and had families of their own. They left the disembodied conversations, the missing silverware, and the scampering, growling thing. Neither the Sherlocks nor their children ever felt threatened by the paranormal occurrences in their home—but the grandchildren have. Something, maybe the ghost of a little boy, has spoken to all eleven grandchildren, has played with them all, and has bullied and terrorized them all. "The grandkids [when they were ages] one to two-and-a-half . . . they've all seen it," McFee said. "And they all say the same thing: 'Little boy. Nightmare. He tried to take my toy.' And it was in the same bedroom." Durbin has more than a cursory interest with this little boy—this nightmare—she heard her son talk with it. "My son, Brad, he was only two so he doesn't remember it," Durbin reports. "He had a conversation with it and called it David. He was in the other room taking a nap. You'd hear him ask a question and answer a question." Durbin and her husband only heard part of Brad's conversation, but Brad was interacting with someone. "I said, 'Who are you talking to?'" Durbin recounts. "And he said, 'David.' We asked where David went and he pointed toward a wall."

Brad wasn't afraid of David, but most of the Sherlocks' grandchildren were because they didn't see a little boy, they saw a monster. Sherlock said, "The little ones, they're two or three, have become petrified and have said, 'It's right there. Can't you see that monster?'" The entity may have appeared as a monster to Brad, too, but that didn't bother him. "Shortly after that he saw something on TV or in a book, and he said, 'That's David,'" McFee said. "The picture was something scary." Even when the visage is of the boy and not a monster, it's not friendly. "They say he takes toys from them," Durbin relates. "The youngest two said he growled at them all the time."

It has been mostly children under the age of three who have experienced the sightings, but one night Durbin, then in her early twenties and pregnant, saw it too. "I was getting up one night and he was standing in front of this picture and he was dressed in knickers—brown—and a white shirt and he was blonde." The visitation didn't last long, less than a minute, but it was long enough for Durbin to remember vividly. "It scared me," she said. Although the entity—be it little boy or monster—has never harmed any member of the Sherlock family, it is still a subject they tread upon lightly.

McFee became concerned enough about the thing, or things, haunting her parents' house that she contacted a medium—and the medium told her the furry creature and David (she called him David without a prompt) aren't the only things haunting the Sherlock house. "The [medium] told me another ghost there died in battle," McFee said. "He's a rough, tough kind a guy. He's there to stay and we can't make him get out. She said the little boy was lost before he died, and there is a woman figure there who takes care of him. She said the little boy is happy with us. He likes our family." But the family doesn't like the little boy and no one is very happy with the other spirits. "The other kids are scared of [David]," Durbin said. "Other than the kids, Michelle's seen the [soldier]. Someone said they saw

3

the woman staring through the window at her." What McFee asserts the family wants now is to simply know what happened to whatever is in the house. "Maybe [the little boy] was a missing child or he was murdered, [the medium] didn't know," she said. "I just want to know what happened to the boy. Everybody gets freaked out, but if we know what happened to him we wouldn't be afraid anymore."

2

A Haunted Campus

Where there are teenagers, there is angst. Where there is angst, there is turmoil. Where there is turmoil, there is often tragedy. University campuses, home to thousands of teenaged and young adult students, are unfortunately and unavoidably homes to such tragedy. A car accident, a drunken rage, a sad decision late one night when roommates are out, a failing grade on your mind, or an old girlfriend haunting your thoughts. Deaths are not uncommon in the halls of higher education, and sometimes these victims of accidents or angst never return home again.

The Northwest Missouri State University campus, a usually tranquil garden of well-trimmed grass that stretches under the 1,300 trees of this state arboretum, is home to its share of triumphs—including three Division II football national championships. But it is the tragedy that lingers long after the seasons are over and the students have gone home for summer. As at any school, students have died while attending Northwest Missouri State University, but here some still walk down its majestic halls.

Franken Hall

Katie Pierce moved into her fourth floor dorm room the Friday before 2007 classes started. This was her sophomore year—she had a job, a spot on the yearbook staff, and, best yet, no roommate. She went home to Nebraska for the weekend and came back to find she didn't have the room to herself after all. Pierce says, "When I first moved in, it was really damp in the room and it had a different smell to it. An old smell." A friend, Harrison Sissel, noticed the smell, too. "He said, 'It's a fragrance,'" Pierce relates. "It wasn't my perfume. I didn't know if it was something or nothing." Rachel Ost, a student from Kansas City,

Missouri, once lived a couple floors down from Pierce in room 201 and she too smelled something odd in her room. "I'd hear things and I'd smell things," she said. "I'd get whiffs of manly cologne. I don't wear a lot of fragrance and I know it wasn't what I was wearing at the time."

During Pierce's first week in her new room, it was nothing. The second week, she realized something else was there with her. Pierce remembers, "I felt a presence in my room. It's almost oppressive. The feeling I get, I just feel tense all the time. When I feel the presence I start looking over my shoulder a lot. It's hard to go to sleep." Pierce sees things in the corner of her eyes—things that move and vanish when she

It starts with a whiff of cologne or a sweet, musty smell—then some residents of Franken Hall awake to find a black shadowy figure looming over their bed.

6

turns to face them. She sleeps with covers up to her neck. "I get these images in my mind," she said. "It's a guy. It's a shadow peering over the side of my bed. It's a loft bed so you'd have to be as tall as the room. It was just dark, but it was definitely a form. I could see eyes, nose, and mouth. I just couldn't see the details. I know I would freak out if I saw something, but seeing something in my head is just as bad."

Pierce hears creaking during the night that she cannot explain away as neighbors or sagging floors. "You know how a laptop sounds when you open and close it?" she asked. "It sounds like someone is messing with my computer but they're not. Then I just hear random noise. It is in my room. Not next door, not upstairs, not in the hallway." Pierce flips on her lamp when she hears these noises, but has never seen anything out of the ordinary. And she only feels the presence when she is alone—but not just when she is in her room. A small common room sits between Pierce's room and her floor's women's bathroom. She hates going through the common room at night, but sometimes nature forces her. "The light [in the common room] is usually turned off when I walk through that room to go to the bathroom," she explains. "I always feel like someone's following me when I leave my room. I still feel the presence in the women's bathroom. It's still a very male presence. I don't know how I know that. I just do." Like Pierce, Ost felt she was being watched during her time in Franken Hall and, occasionally she would hear a knock on her door. "There was no one there," she said. "There was no one in the hallway. A lot of times I didn't go home on weekends, and this always happened in the middle of the weekend."

Sissel's girlfriend lives on the fifth floor of the dorm and when he uses the men's bathroom on her floor—directly above the women's bathroom Pierce uses—he can't see anyone there, but he knows he is never alone. "The bathroom's empty except for me and it sounds like someone unzips their pants, but nothing happens, and you hear it zip back up," he said. "I've looked [into the stalls] and no one is in there. I've also heard jingling keys in the men's bathroom. I'm the only one in there."

Ghosts are usually associated with a violent or unexpected death. In December 2005, Shawn Bussey, a twenty-one-year-old male student from Springfield, Missouri, died of diabetic shock in Pierce's dormitory

7

two floors beneath her room. According to a news report, "Bussey was found dead in his Franken Hall dorm room where he lived alone."

Michael Willis, a broadcasting major, lives next to Pierce and said he has not heard or experienced anything paranormal. And Evan Young, a journalism major, lives in the room where Bussey died. He also says his room is quiet. "I picked it because, hey, 214, the Valentine suite," Young said. "Then I found someone died there." But he has not experienced anything out of the ordinary. "If I do I'll have you on speed dial," Young added. This doesn't make Pierce feel any better. She just wants to be left alone. "All I know is it's a guy and I don't know what he wants," she said. "I don't want to piss it off. I don't want to talk with it. I just want to coexist. I don't like to talk about what's going on when I'm in my room. I hate the dark."

Phillips Hall

The dormitory was quiet the night Resident Assistant (RA) Shane Sherwood, his friend Rachel Ost, and a smattering of others were posting homemade decorations on doors welcoming new students to the university. Students would arrive in a few days—on August 26, 2007—but as Sherwood and Ost discovered, someone was already there.

Ost peeled Scotch tape off a roll and attached another piece of colored paper to a door, the rip of the adhesive loud in the lonely hall. Ost was the only person on the floor, an odd enough feeling when in a building that would soon house hundreds of students, but she soon found something was wrong. "Shane and the other RA were on rounds, or something like that," she said. "There was no one on the floor except for me." Nonetheless, something moved and Ost froze as she watched it move past her. "I was hanging up door decs and there's this pair of legs," she said. "This pair of legs runs by. No torso. There's just feet. I said, 'What the fuck was that?'" The translucent legs ran down the hallway and disappeared. Although Ost never told Sherwood of the encounter, he would soon meet his new hall mate.

The night before hundreds of freshman would pour into Phillips Hall, Sherwood and the other RAs worked to finish posting door decorations. Sherwood was alone on the sixth floor, the only other person authorized to be on the floor was his fellow RA, but he was on the opposite

8

A ghost—sometimes only seen as a running pair of legs—stalks the floors of Phillips Hall. Residents believe it's the spirit of a student who died in a car accident in 1999.

side of the building and out of sight. That's when Sherwood saw someone move. "I just saw something walk behind me," he recalled. He looked around, but there was no one in the hallway. Sherwood started looking into the nearby rooms and found nothing—until he walked toward the open door of room 626. Something there was different. The windows in the room, like in all rooms in the dormitory, were closed and the air conditioning was still off for the summer, but the air in room 626 was cold—cold enough to staple a note onto Sherwood's memory. He quickly realized someone was there. "I went into room 626 and there was somebody sitting in the corner," Sherwood said. "I couldn't really make out his face." Startled, he backed away from the room and its inhabitant, and went to find Phillips Hall director Aimee Rea. "I went to see if she knew anything about it," he said. And she told him the story.

In April 1999, Northwest student and Phillips Hall resident Kevin Bayer, 19, of Sutton, Nebraska, died from injuries received in a car accident, according to the campus newspaper archives. And, according to the story passed from RA to RA over the years, Bayer is supposed to haunt the dormitory. Rea said it is people who keep the

9

ghost story around, not a ghost. She is not convinced the story is true. "Supposedly, his spirit resides in the halls and spends a lot of time in the [hall director] apartment," she said. "I have not experienced anything paranormal and believe that my friends made up the stories just to see if I would get spooked." But people have encountered strange things in Phillips Hall, like cabinets opening and shutting on their own, pets reacting to something their owners cannot see, and the feeling of being watched. Like Sherwood, many people have reported seeing Bayer's ghost. "There's a picture downstairs in the trophy case of a student who died in a car crash," Sherwood said. "He was wearing the same clothes as the guy I saw."

Wells Hall
Deep concrete and brick stairwells lead into the basement of Wells Hall. This thick structure, built as a library in 1939, is almost sound-less as you walk its halls, tricking students and faculty in the building after hours into thinking they are there alone—they never are. Mold built up over seventy years drifts through the air of this structure that houses the Departments of Mass Communication, Speech Communi-cation, and Foreign Language. And in the basement home of Student Publications, it also houses the ghost of Amos Wong who, like the mold, is somehow imbedded in the old library.

Dominic Genetti, a reporter for the student newspaper, *The Northwest Missourian*, was sitting in the newsroom when he saw Amos in 2008. "I turned and looked out the corner of my eye and I could have sworn I saw somebody in a button-down blue shirt," he said. "Not a royal blue, just blue. And I couldn't really get the body type out of it, but it was definitely a person I saw walk by in jeans." When Genetti looked directly, he expected someone to turn the cor-ner toward him, but no one did. "I walked into the hallway and there's no one in the basement," he said. "There were times in the Conver-gence Lab that the light above me will flicker. There will be a reflection in the Mac computer that looked like someone walked behind me. And I looked behind me and no one was there." The Convergence Lab is special—before digital cameras, it was the darkroom.

Wong, a photographer for the school yearbook, *the Tower*, died

Amos Wong, a photographer who died in 1991, sometimes visits student employees of NWMSU's publications, with offices in the basement of Wells Hall.

in a 1991 car accident as he traveled to California to visit his parents. Assistant Professor Laura Widmer, student publication adviser, said Wong joined the yearbook staff because of his passion for photography. "He was just on staff for a year," Widmer said. "He was an international student [who] enjoyed photography and joined the yearbook staff. He was a [happy-]go-lucky kind of guy. Wouldn't hurt anyone. Just a little mischievousness in his eye."

But it wasn't long after Wong's death that student publication staffers began to notice something strange in the basement. A student who had worked on staff with Wong told Widmer, "You know, Amos is back in the darkroom." Widmer said, "I'm not sure he ever saw Amos, but there are things like music going on and lights going on. Just strange

11

occurrences. Photographers would say there was someone in the dark-room with them. It just felt like someone." Scott Jenson, Northwest graduate and journalism adviser for Platteview High School in Spring-field, Nebraska, worked with Wong on the yearbook staff and said Wong's personality might have kept him around. "Once he broke out of his shell he was one of the guys," Jenson said. "We spent many evenings in the darkroom so there [were] always jokes and pranks going on. I will agree with Laura that he was a great kid and mischievous."

But current students don't see Wong that way. *Tower* editor-in-chief Katie Pierce gets "creeped out" in the Wells Hall basement, and Genetti is uncomfortable alone in the bowels of the building. "There are times where you just get that feeling you don't want to go to the other end of the basement," Genetti said, nodding toward the Convergence Lab. "There are times I just don't want to go down there." At certain times of day, sunlight shines though the door and brightens Amos's photo on an award in his honor, a reminder to all that Amos is still around. "I don't want to walk through the dark," Genetti said. "I just get that feeling. I just don't want to do it when you know the history of that stuff down there."

Roberta Hall

The red brick sorority house called Roberta Hall stands at the east edge of campus. The hall wasn't always a sorority house and it wasn't always called Roberta. In the early days it was the only women's residence hall on campus and was simply known as Residence Hall. That changed after the explosion. Railroad tracks once ran behind the building, and on April 28, 1951, a gasoline storage tank on the tracks exploded, sending a steel beam crashing into the building and causing a fire. Thirty women were injured, four of them critically, including a student named Roberta Steel. "Roberta was in the shower when the explosion hit," Cathy Palmer, archivist at Northwest, said. "She wouldn't come out for help because she was naked." Roberta died from problems related to her injuries a year and a half later and, over the decades, her spirit is said to haunt the building.

Student Rachel Ost knows Roberta is there—she has felt her. Late one night, Ost was on rounds with a friend who was a resident

Residents of Roberta Hall are convinced the ghost of Roberta Steel, who died in 1951, roams the building that bears her name.

assistant when she met Roberta. Ost tells, "We went through Roberta [Hall] and I felt this tap on the back of my shoulders," she said. "There was no one there." At first Ost blamed it on her imagination, but Roberta would not be ignored. "We went down to the basement and my hair got pulled," Ost said. "Not hard, but it did get pulled." After that, she tread more cautiously. As Ost and her friend walked through the downstairs common room, a portrait of Roberta that stares out from the wall seemed to glare at her. "The eyes followed me," she said, "which creeped me out considerably."

Linda Beatty of Kansas City attended Northwest from 1984 to 1988 and lived in Roberta Hall in 1987. "I was on the first floor," Linda said. "[My roommate and I] were just lying there watching TV … and we heard the crickety old doorknob move. We thought someone was coming in." Linda even called, "come in," but no one did—and they saw

13

the doorknob keep turning. Linda said, "I got frustrated and opened the door and there was no one there." Then Linda turned the doorknob on the hallway side of the door. That doorknob moved. The doorknob inside the room did not. "Somebody was moving the doorknob on the inside," she said. Jane Costello (who died in 2005) went to school with Roberta and thought the legend of the haunting was fitting. "She was lots of fun," Jane said in a summer 2000 interview for Northwest's Oral History program. "She's being credited with the scaring—the haunting of Roberta Hall—and I had to laugh because you know if anybody's going to do it, it would be Roberta. She had a really terrific sense of humor."

Sarah Wayman, who graduated from Northwest in 2005, was a member of Sigma Kappa sorority and lived in Roberta Hall from fall 2002 to spring 2003. Sarah said that although she only experienced flickering lights and strange noises while she lived there, Roberta got the blame for anything out of the ordinary. "Anything wrong that happened was blamed on Roberta," Sarah said. "We discovered one morning that, hey, we can't get in our bathroom. We called each other saying 'Did you lock the door to the bathroom?'" They couldn't have, because the doors locked on the inside. "We blamed it on Roberta."

Towels fall off their racks in Roberta Hall, pictures fall off the wall, stereos turn on and off, and drawers fly from dressers. Amanda Root, former president of the Phi Mu sorority, lived in Roberta Hall for two years before graduating in 2006. "I was looking in the mirror getting ready and I saw my roommate's drawer shoot out of the dresser and it really kind of scared me," she said. "I turned and was like 'what the hell was that?' I grabbed my bag and left." But the flying drawer wasn't enough to prepare her for an unwelcome late-night visitor. "I had gotten up because I'd heard someone walking around and I thought it was my roommate, but I looked over and she was in bed," Amanda said. "I hadn't encountered anything like that but when I heard somebody walking around, it really freaked me out. Our floor is really squeaky. I was really scared. I put the covers over my head."

Although Roberta has never harmed anyone, many sorority sisters have tried a wide variety of things over the years to keep her out of their rooms, but to no avail. Roberta continues to make herself known to residents of the hall that bears her name.

3

Something Fell from the Sky

Checkerboard fields, painted green, gold, or brown by the season, cover the soft hills of Nodaway County in northwest Missouri. But in winter, as the sky sprinkles snow across the county, fields become uniform: cold, dead, and uninviting. A field just outside Skidmore looks the same as any of its neighbors. Former farmhand Bruce Sanders walks through the white December dust that hides the dark clods of disc-turned earth that would, in a few months, sprout life. As a boy and into early adulthood Sanders worked for Bill Ruddell, who owned this field until his death in the 1990s. Sanders knows that the old Ruddell field near Burr Oak Road off state Route 46 is different from its neighbors. Sanders walked to a spot, about ten feet in diameter, which still dips into the field next to a fencerow. "Huh," he said, moving around the perimeter of the circular dent in the ground, "It's still here." The spot—a crater—has been in the field since July 9, 1979, when something came screaming out of the sky and crashed into a sea of soybeans. Sanders was surprised the crater was still visible because thirty years ago he had plowed the spot over.

Summers in Midwest farm country crawl with teenagers wearing leather gloves who stalk soybean fields with hoes or corn knifes, swinging death to the sunflower, cottonweed, and cocklebur plants threatening to rob the rows and rows of soybeans of valuable sunlight and moisture. Sanders, now a cattle rancher near Elmo, Missouri, was fifteen years old and living in Skidmore when he and his brothers walked through a swath of scorched soybean plants in Ruddell's field to find something they couldn't have expected. "We

15

Something fell from the sky in 1979 and smashed into this soybean field, killing only weeds, but causing the beans to grow abnormally large.

came to a depression in the ground," Sanders said. "It was like a small bomb went off. Everything was smooth as glass there." The depression was a crater ten to fourteen feet across and from two to three feet deep, growing deeper toward the center. As the boys waded through waist-high soybeans toward the crater, they noticed the beans were scorched. "Not burn marks," Sanders stated. "No black burns. The soybeans looked like they were chemical burned, not with fire."

When Sanders and his brothers came across the hole, "We were like, what in the world?" From the object's trail, the boys figured it had streaked through the sky from the south almost parallel to the field's fence, scarred the soybean plants on entry, struck the earth, and scorched soybean plants to the north as it skipped back into the sky. "From where the indention is and where the scorch marks were, that's the direction you could see where it went," Sanders said. "Where it took off and crested the hill, it burned the soybeans as it [came] up across the hill. It disappeared. It was like it shot into space and that was the end of it." Shortly after Sanders found the crater, Ruddell called Roger Cronk, Nodaway County sheriff from 1976 to 1980, and asked him to take a look at it. "I said 'sure,'" Cronk, now of Moravia, Iowa, reported. "There was evidence of a burn mark in a circular area on the ground where Bill thought this thing, whatever it was, landed." The men discussed the possibility of a craft landing and taking off. "Any [disturbed] ground was [from] the weight of the machine setting down on the ground," Cronk said, although he stopped short of claiming the machine was a UFO. "It was something we didn't deal with on a regular basis. I'll just put it that way."

Journalist Marli Murphy, now a columnist with *The Kansas City Star*, covered the incident as a reporter for *The Maryville Daily Forum*. "The [beans] had been burnt back to scorched earth, and the ground had been made hard, as if by a really high heat," Murphy said. "The farmer was convinced that something had entered the ground with great force and heat. Or at the very least, something blazingly hot had touched down and then, well, gone away however it came."

Ruddell and Sanders combed that area and neighboring fields to find anything left of the object, but found nothing. "Seems like anything heavy enough to make this hole would still be here," Ruddell stated in Murphy's July 11, 1979, article. "We never found any debris of any way, shape, or form," Sanders said. "We looked [over] the entire bean field, the next wheat field, and the pasture. Bill owned all of them. Government people came and looked. Nobody ever came up with anything. It was just a bizarre deal."

The brothers walked to the crater and saw that the dent in the earth was peppered with a bluish-silver powder and small circular holes shooting straight into the ground. "When we arrived there, it had silver-lined holes about the size of a man's finger," Sanders said. "There were several. We dug into it and they were like perfect holes straight into the ground." It was the holes that most fascinated Sanders. "You couldn't dig down and find the bottom of them," he explains. "But to be honest with you, we didn't know what it was and we probably shouldn't have been digging in it." Someone, Sanders remembers, speculated whatever made the crater buried itself there and exploded underground. "And those were the vent holes," he said. "How dumb do you think we are? These holes were straight up. They didn't tilt. That's the part that got people; they were so perfect."

Although Sanders doesn't remember how many holes were in the crater, he remembers the powder: "There were numerous holes and they had some silvery substance. I don't know how to tell you what it was because we didn't know and nobody gave us a good answer later."

Dr. James Smeltzer, an astronomy professor at Northwest Missouri State University in nearby Maryville, gathered some of the slivery powder and was given a clod that, according to a newspaper article, was "smooth and had a trace of something like hardened paint on it." But whatever Smeltzer discovered about the powder or clod—whether they be of a known or unknown substance—is gone with him. Smeltzer died in 2006 and neither his widow nor his former department at the university have any record of the analysis of the powder left in the Ruddell field. Neither does nearby Offutt Air Force Base, which sent investigators to survey the crater. A Freedom of Information Act (FOIA) request generated no records on an Offutt Air Force Base investigation of the incident, although the 1979 article in *The Maryville Daily Forum* states, "officials from Offutt Air Force Base in Omaha" had been sent to examine the spot. The FOIA report, however, plainly stated there were no records indicating a military aircraft could have been responsible for the impact. *The Forum* article stated Ruddell thought the Air Force "may be reluctant to admit a piece of a plane or spacecraft caused the hole," not because of a national security problem, but because he felt the government was worried he might sue "for damages."

A local Air Force man, Bud King, who is now deceased, inspected the scene and was convinced the crater was caused by a fuel tank falling off an airplane. The Skidmore area is under an air highway between Kansas City, Missouri, and Omaha, Nebraska. "Bud King came up there and looked at it," Sanders said. "He was a retired colonel and he lived between Maitland and Skidmore. He said it was a 55-gallon drum out of the back of an airplane. It could have exploded." But further FOIA requests showed the FAA does not have record of anything falling from, or off, a civilian aircraft on July 9, 1979.

Sanders agrees that part of an aircraft would not have caused what he found in the soybean field. A piece of a jet engine once fell onto a field on his property near Elmo and hit the ground intact, the majority of it sticking above the surface. The object that made the crater "could not have fallen off a plane," Sanders asserts. Smeltzer eventually contacted NASA to see if a piece of man-made space debris could have caused the crater. *The Maryville Daily Forum* reported, "NASA representatives told Smeltzer that while no pieces of man-made crafts were reported falling to earth over Missouri ... pieces of space stations or space exploration vehicles fall to earth someplace almost every day." Fifteen-year-old Sanders speculated the crater may have been caused by a falling piece of Skylab I. The space station's decaying orbit had made international headlines and, two days after something struck the Ruddell field, Skylab I broke up as it re-entered Earth's atmosphere, scattering pieces across the Indian Ocean and Western Australia.

Once the story came out in *The Forum*, the media flooded Skidmore. "Hoards of reporters came," Sanders recounts. "ABC, NBC came out." Which then brought more attention to Ruddell's small farm than he wanted. "There [were] all kind of nuts that came out there during the night and tried to dig," Sanders said. "They were trying to look for meteors or aliens. It got nutty." Day and night, UFO hunters showed up in Ruddell's field. "It was kind of a running joke," Sanders said. "Aliens. But there were people who didn't think of it as a joke. Bill and I were both on the same page. We can't explain it, but it's here. Bill would have hated to say it was a UFO."

Then, as the attention from the media and UFO hunters began to wane, something happened in Ruddell's soybean field that was even stranger than the mysterious creation of the crater. "It made the beans grow dramatically after this," Sanders said. "The beans were nice beans at the time, but they just burst." In the area surrounding the impact crater, the soybeans soon began to tower over bean plants in the rows around them. "The first year almost immediately it grew," Sanders said. "I wouldn't say it doubled the size of the surrounding beans, but it was close." But something else happened in the immediate vicinity of the crater. "It killed all the cockleburs and all the weeds died," Sanders said. "You couldn't have had the kill rate with whatever this was with cockleburs and sunflowers. Bill and I joked if we could just get that into a bottle and sell it to Monsanto..."

Whatever crashed into Bill Ruddell's soybean field on July 9, 1979, is still a mystery, one that thrust itself on people who didn't want it. "I remember the farmer didn't strike me as weird or bizarre. Not at all," Murphy said. "Just a run-of-the-mill old farmer who had something odd happen in the middle of a field, and he wanted to know more than anyone what had happened." Although it has been more than thirty years since the incident, Sanders rarely talks about it. "It's one of those things I can't explain," he said. "I've probably not mentioned this to about five people in my life because they make fun of it."

4

Workman Chapel

Deep gray clouds masked the setting sun as the cars pulled into Workman Chapel's dirt drive, which split the cornfields pouring across the hills of northwest Missouri. Seven people were on the ghost hunt: me, audiovisual engineer Will Murphy, and five Northwest Missouri State University students. We parked under the limbs of two trees grown old next to the chapel. According to legend, a woman was hanged from one of those trees, and anyone sitting in a car beneath it hears her shoes scraping on the roof of the car. Only a legend, yes, but the students were still nervous. Workman Chapel, quiet in the dusk, stared at us from black, glassless windows. We were there to find the ghosts of the hanged woman and two Civil War soldiers who reportedly ride their horses in the chapel's cemetery.

Pastor John Workman built the chapel in 1901. His descendent Lester Workman is caretaker of the chapel. "It's been empty for years," he said. "It's been fifty years or better." People have heard church bells peal at the chapel—although there is no bell—and have seen black, human shapes dancing on the tombstones. That's what we wanted to experience. I could see from the broken bottles and crushed beer cans scattered across the chapel floor and dirt driveway that high school and college kids play here. But do ghosts? Lester doesn't think so, and he's not sure the hanging ever happened. Lester said, "There's supposed to be a murder or hanging out west here," but "I don't know whether there was or whether there wasn't."

Will, an engineer from Northwest Missouri State University's Department of Mass Communication, brought digital cameras, a digital video camera, a digital audio recorder, and a voltmeter. The cameras were to capture orbs—balls of light people rarely see with

This ghostly white band that encircles NWMSU student Bria Gardner was present in only one of three consecutive shots taken at Workman Chapel Cemetery.

their eyes but that appear in digital pictures. Some people claim these orbs, which didn't start appearing regularly in photographs until the profusion of digital cameras, are pictures of ghosts. Others say they are light reflecting off dust, insects, or moisture—and most of the time they are. The video and audio equipment were to record disembodied shadows and voices. The concept of capturing voices of ghosts, known as electronic voice phenomena or EVPs, has been around since the time of Thomas Edison, who once told a reporter he was working on a machine that would allow him to speak to the dead.

Freshmen Kayla Lindsey, Katie Pierce, and Harrison Sissel shot still pictures in the dark cemetery, while Mallory Riley wandered with the voltmeter, trying to pick up energy fluctuations some associate with ghosts. Then the fun began. Katie and Kayla called me over. Katie has just taken two pictures. One has orbs. The other doesn't. If dust, insects, or moisture caused the orbs, they should have been in both pictures—they're not. Did Katie capture the image of a ghost? Who knows? "Oh my God," Kayla whispered as Mallory passes by with the voltmeter. Will said the meter generally picks up fourteen volts out of the air; more near an electrical source. If the meter went past forty,

Mallory is supposed to tell us. "It's gone up to eighty," announced Kayla, shining a flashlight on the meter. Ninety. One hundred. One hundred and fifteen. The meter reaches one hundred and twenty before Will points out that the students are walking toward utility lines. Rookie mistake.

After several hours Harrison runs into one of the great problems of ghost hunting in a mixed crowd. He has to use the bathroom and doesn't want to go alone. Kayla laughs, "He can't pee in front of ghosts." Maybe it was time to go.

Did we find evidence of ghosts? The orbs were interesting, but inconclusive and debatable. We didn't pick up any voices on our recordings. And we didn't detect anomalous energy fields. But others have experienced things at Workman Chapel that we can't explain.

<hr />

I met the teenage girls at the Maryville Community Center right before their basketball game. Gathered in a pack that junior high school boys would fear if they had ever watched a lion documentary on the Discovery Channel, they giggled as I approached. "Are you Jason?" one of them asked. "Yes," I said. Then they squealed in a pitch audible only to dolphins and bats. But the girls—Mary Beth Seipel, Rachel Tobin, Mataya Wooten, Molly Stiens, Kylie Stiens, and Traci Shipps—had reason to be excited. On October 7, 2006, the girls, at the time seventh and eighth graders, had talked two of their moms, Kim Stiens and Karla Wooten, into driving them to Workman Chapel on a ghost hunt—and something unexplainable happened.

Kim and Karla took the girls to the chapel between nine and ten o'clock at night to experience something none of the girls could agree on. "The seventh grade teacher got online and said that Workman was one of the most haunted places," Kylie said. Mataya interrupts, "In Maryville." So Kylie speaks louder, "No, in Nodaway County." "A kid hung himself in the chapel," Mataya added. "No," Kylie said. "In the tree."

For the record, it was in the tree.

To prime themselves, Mataya brought a movie to play on the DVD player in Karla's 2005 Toyota Sienna. "I have *The Exorcism of*

23

Emily Rose. We wanted to watch it to scare us," she explained. "When we finally arrived at Workman Chapel, we took the movie out [of the DVD player] and sat it on the floor because we couldn't find the case." Kim pulled onto the chapel grounds and backed under one of the large, crooked trees looming toward the chapel. Molly said, "We thought it looked like a hand." After Kim put the vehicle in park, "the girls screamed and we got out. The moon was full that night. We decided to take some pictures with the full moon," Kim said. "But the girls wanted to go to the cemetery."

They walked through the cemetery for a couple of minutes. Karla tells, "We saw headlights coming down the road and Kim said they were coming into the chapel." The girls ran. "It looked like the headlights were coming our way," Kim said. "They [the girls] were screaming." But the cemetery and the headlights wouldn't be the biggest scare of the night—it was *The Exorcism of Emily Rose*.

"Before we got out of the car and put the movie on the floor, I asked them to close the [television] screen," Kim said. Did they? "It was off," Rachel said. The girls were laughing as they threw themselves into the car, until the GPS screen displayed something it couldn't have. "I have a navigation system. When I put it in reverse, the camera comes on to show what was behind you," Kim said. "I'm backing up and I decided I'm going to shove on the brakes and make them think I hit something." But she didn't have to—there was already something there. "I go, 'Oh my God, look,'" Molly said. "Oh my God," Rachel screamed. "Look at the screen." On the GPS screen was something no one expected, and why would they? It wasn't possible. "It was the part of the movie when Emily Rose is walking through the cemetery toward the little tree," Mataya said. The movie was still on the floor, the DVD player was off. According to Angela at the Toyota Customer Experience Center, the DVD player (which faces the back seat) and Toyota Navigation System (in the dash) are connected, but under the circumstances the movie couldn't have played. "If the DVD wasn't in the player, then no, it shouldn't have," Angela said. "I think we all got chills thinking about it," Karla said.

Cody Maser of Maryville got chills there, too. Cody was sixteen when he visited Workman Chapel with his sister Ashley. "We went straight under the tree and as always we heard what we thought were feet scraping against the rooftop of the car," he said. "But it was different this time. We heard three or four different people's feet scraping against the roof and heard people gasping, trying to breathe." Ashley started the car and they left ... but not for long. "We wanted to see if it would happen again, so we turned around and went back." The car's temperature gauge began to dance as she pulled back into the chapel's dirt drive ... then they had a visitor. "Just then a truck came from the highway the way you come in to come to Workman Chapel, and we were just sitting there and this beat-up junky-looking truck came in right behind us and bright-lighted the car like he was searching it," Cody said. "Then he backed out of the driveway and sped out of there like a bat out of hell." The kids had had enough and sped back into Maryville. "When we got to some lights we stopped and got out and looked at the top of the car," Cody said. "And there [were] marks like shoes making a black mark when you scrape them on tile."

Who was in the "beat-up junky-looking truck?" Cody may have met someone Brooke Breason of nearby Hopkins, Missouri, knows as "Mike." She met Mike on October 31, 2004, and hopes to never see him again. Brooke and a few friends were walking through the cemetery ghost hunting when Mike showed up. "We were reading off names from tombstones to see if we'd get a reaction [from the spirits]," she said. "I thought, 'whatever.' Every college student makes a big deal of it if they're not from around here." Nothing happened until Brooke and her friends decided to go home around midnight. "We were getting ready to leave and we see these headlights come from the road," she said. "We thought, 'Crap, there are high school kids here for a party.'" But the person who pulled up in a beat-up junky-looking truck wasn't a high school kid. "We peek around the corner and all of a sudden we hear this old guy yelling," she said. "This guy looked like he came out of the 1930s—long beard. He said, 'What are you doing here? This is disrespectful.'" And he had an axe. "He said 'F' this and 'F' that. He chased us back to our cars," Brooke said. A small, mousy woman had gotten out of the truck and stood next to the wild man. "A soft voice called him Mike. You hear of people hearing footsteps and random cold spots but you don't hear people getting chased with an axe." Brooke and her friends quickly left the chapel, the cemetery, Mike, and the soft voice, but they still wonder who he is. "He was seriously pissed off," she said. "What was weird was we'd just read a tombstone for a Michael." Who is Michael? Caretaker Lester Workman's wife, Daisy, doesn't know. He is certainly not associated with the Workmans or the chapel. "Michael with a beard?" Daisy asked. "Not that we know anything about." Were Brooke and Cody chased off by one of the ghosts of Workman Chapel? Maybe. Or maybe not.

Northwest Missouri State University chemistry and physics professor Dr. Rick Toomey visited Workman Chapel to gather evidence on the existence (or nonexistence) of ghosts. Workman Chapel didn't offer much in the way of quantifiable proof. "I don't think we found anything," Rick said. "We went out about dusk, [a] completely clear night. We were so far away from the highway we could see every star in the sky. Beautiful." They took audio recorders, a video camera, and flashlights. Flashlights are always important … people trip over things in the dark. "We walked around the building and went through the cemetery trying to be respectful," Rick said; they attempted to step around graves, not walk over them. "We sat the camera down a couple of times to keep it motionless." After about two hours and fifteen minutes of exploring and recording, the scientists had several things on audio. It was what they expected, just not what they'd hoped. "We went through all the tape and all the video," Rick said. "The tape picked up the crickets, the coyotes, the planes, nothing anomalous. Certainly no EVP." Although the scientists didn't find anything otherworldly at Workman Chapel, Rick confesses this doesn't mean there's nothing out there. "As much as I'm trained to think [as a scientist], there's lots of times I've had the cold chills and the hair on the back of my neck stand up."

5

The Christian House

A patchwork of green, brown, and gold blankets the hills that roll up to Maitland in great smooth waves. Maitland isn't an old town (established in 1880), and with a population of 342, it isn't a large town. The main industry is agriculture, made apparent by the sea of fields and pastures that surround Maitland, and the town's largest building, which houses Maitland Grain and Feed. Time has long since flaked the white paint off the old brick buildings downtown. Some of these buildings still see activity, such as the Opera-House Tavern, the senior center, and the Farmers State Bank, but dark, empty windows stare from the dusty front rooms of most buildings. However, an old, two-story family farmhouse about one-half mile outside Maitland sees more activity than any building in town.

Bob Christian's family doesn't live in the farmhouse anymore, but the memories made there still live with them. "Our old house is haunted," Christian said. "There can be no other explanation for all the things that have happened over the years." Christian, now in his sixties, was much younger when his family moved into the two-story house. It wasn't long before Christian and his mother both experienced things they couldn't explain. "When I was a young man I saw the door knob turning to the door of my bedroom upstairs and the door swung open about an inch all by itself," he said. "I opened the door and there was no one on the other side of the door. Often my mother and I both felt like someone was watching us." Years later when Christian was in the army, his mother saw that, yes, over the years something had been watching them. "My mother opened the stair door and started to go upstairs, and saw a man and a woman standing at the top of the stairs looking down at her," Christian said.

"They were dressed in 1800s clothes. They disappeared right in front of her eyes. She refused to go upstairs again till the day she died. She said that the upstairs always felt sad."

His parents later moved to a house within the city limits of Maitland, and Christian moved into the old house with his wife and six children. Although his wife never experienced anything strange, their children did. "My three daughters slept upstairs and always complained that the covers were pulled off of them in the middle of the night by some invisible force," Christian said. "One daughter said that she woke up one night to see a woman bending over her pulling at her covers and telling her to hurry and get up." And once, whoever— whatever—existed in the old house became violent toward one of Christian's children. Christian's 6' 2" son was lying in a bed upstairs. He was on his back with his hand and forearm in the air "bent like you would have it bent for arm wrestling," Christian said, when something attacked him. "Something grabbed his arm and started forcing it down against the mattress. He could not stop it with all his strength, though he is very strong. It was arm wrestling with him and put his arm down against the mattress like he was nothing. He jumped up and turned on the light and there was no one there."

Human-shaped shadows have walked through the living room; ink pens have flown through the air; phantom footsteps have slapped through the night; and stools have scooted across the floor upstairs. "We would hear the wooden stool slide across the floor and we would rush upstairs to find it upside down or something," Christian said. "My three sons would set it on a certain spot on the floor and mark on the floor where each of the legs sat on the floor and by bedtime it would have moved from several feet to all the way across the room."

Although many of these occurrences caused Christian to search the house with a .38-caliber pistol, he never found a terrestrial explanation—but he did find an unearthly one. "I think something must have happened on this homestead in early history because I found an old pistol still cocked as if ready to fire," Christian said. "I found it about three inches under our yard with my metal detector." Christian also found charcoal where an old cabin burned down, a flint striker, and other pioneer artifacts he dates to around the 1840s. "The pistol and the artifacts were something that an old-timer would not have given up unless he was killed," Christian said. "There was a large Indian summer encampment about three miles south of here, and I have a theory that some pioneers homesteaded here and were killed by the Indians, but can't prove it. I don't know if it is their ghosts haunting this old place or [someone else's], but me and my whole family believe this place to be haunted. There are just too many things that have happened here that can't be explained."

6

Mike Marcum's Time Machine

Almost 1,300 people live in Stanberry, a town shaded with tall, leafy trees. Cannons sit in the city park, Rainey's Supermarket boasts an ATM, and a convenience store offers gasoline, pizza, and fishing worms. People standing next to you at the gas pump smile and say "Good morning." No "pay before you pump" here; people are too polite for that.

But it wasn't courtesy, park cannons, pizza, or fishing worms that put the country's focus on Stanberry in the mid-1990s. It was what happened in a white house at 401 East Third Street, its paint now peeling under the punishment of Missouri weather. In 1995, Mike Marcum, a young man from Cincinnati (Ohio) who was renting the house, claimed that he had accomplished something H. G. Wells popularized in 1895: he claimed to have built a time machine. Marcum disappeared a few years later, leaving paranormal talk radio hosts and bloggers to speculate, "Where in the world is Mike Marcum?" But considering the nature of Marcum's hobby, the question should be "*When* in the world is Mike Marcum?"

Marcum, a twenty-one-year-old with two years of college-level electrical training at Rio Grande College in Rio Grande, Ohio, didn't start out intending to build a time machine—things just turned out that way. Marcum built a Jacob's ladder—two metal rods with a spark going between them—on his kitchen table in December 1994. In the old black-and-white movies, one of these babies helped bring Frankenstein's monster to life. And, like Dr. Frankenstein, when Marcum turned on his Jacob's ladder, something big happened. "Right

In 1995, a twenty-one-year-old former electrical school student claimed to have built a time machine in this Stanberry house. Friends in nearby St. Joseph haven't seen him since 1999.

above it, it was like a regular heat signature, but it was kinda like circular shaped in the center," Marcum said in a 1995 interview with paranormal talk show host Art Bell. "At first I didn't know what it was. I'm not 100 percent certain now." The circle was about the size of a dime, he told The St. Joseph News-Press in 1995, and he did what any guy would have done—he threw something at it. "I put a sheet metal screw through it," he told the News-Press. "It took about a half-second for the screw to disappear and the same amount of time for it to reappear from a foot to eighteen inches away on the table supporting the time machine."

Time machine? Yeah, Marcum was sure he'd built a time machine. The next step? He built a man-sized Jacob's ladder on his porch. "If you can go through it without being killed you can use it as a time machine," he told the News-Press. Marcum wanted to construct a time machine, not to improve life as we know it or to contribute to the body of human knowledge—he wanted to get rich. "I plan to go ahead three or four days to get lottery numbers then use them," Marcum said in 1995. Gentry County Sheriff Eugene Lupfer worked the Marcum case and remembered it well. "That's right," Lupfer said, laughing. "I think he thought he could do it."

But to make his time machine work Marcum needed power. "He stole some transformers," Lupfer said, "and had them hooked up in his house, and he was going to make a time machine." Marcum and a friend stole six transformers—each weighing over three hundred pounds and each capable of producing anywhere from 12,000 to 76,000 volts—from a St. Joseph Light and Power generating station in King City, Missouri. Not in the cover of night, but at 11:00 a.m.

Terry Raymond, Stanberry city manager and lifelong resident, worked in the city's electric department when Marcum made headlines across the country. "The [transformers] were sitting in an electrical substation," Raymond said. "They were in an enclosed, fenced-in area—padlocked."

The city was tipped off to Marcum's experiments when he fired up his machine. "When he turned it on, the houses for blocks would go dim," Lupfer said. "Neighbors called it in. It's a wonder he hadn't blown the whole block up." When Raymond and law enforcement officers entered Marcum's house, the transformers were scattered everywhere. "He had a transformer sitting right in his front room," Raymond said. "The one that drew interest was the one torn apart. We were concerned about PCB [polychlorinated biphenyls] contamination. Suits [people in hazardous material suits] were called in." But the transformers were clean, just stolen, and the one Marcum took apart he'd turned into a piggy bank. "The one he was supposed to be building his time capsule with was right on the back porch," Raymond said. "He had that Jacob's ladder hooked up."

The rental house now sits empty and quiet at the corner of Elm and Third. "I think he was probably the last one who lived in it," Raymond said. Marcum tapped the transformer into the electrical panel on the back porch, a small enclosed porch now crowded with old, broken furniture. Could this dusty, saggy porch be the spot where a twenty-one-year-old college dropout created the greatest invention of humankind? "I don't know," Raymond said. "I think he was just playing around."

The Gentry County Sheriff's Department arrested Marcum

on January 29, 1995, and charged him with a felony, according to the *News-Press*. Marcum pleaded guilty and received five years probation. After serving two months in jail for his crime, Marcum moved to nearby St. Joseph where Claudia Sanderson befriended him. "He always lived alone and spent much of his spare time at the local library and looking for pieces of wire and items he could salvage for his inventions," Sanderson said. "His surroundings were very minimal. He had very little furniture and didn't seem to have many groceries in his place either. We took him groceries and took him out to eat. He was a burger and fries guy, nothing fancy." In St. Joseph, Marcum began to rebuild the time machine—legally this time. Sanderson saw Marcum's Jacob's ladder and other equipment in his apartment kitchen. "It was rather impressive, considering he made workable equipment out of spare parts from other items," she said. "He turned it on and it made the lights dim quite a bit."

Marcum had few friends and was suspicious of everyone, Sanderson said, and although he was a quiet young man, he did talk to Sanderson about his time machine. "He said that his machine worked because he could throw a pencil or pen over or through the electrical field and it would disappear," she recalled. "Then later, an old newspaper from a very long time past and some other objects came through. It was like they were coughed into or out of an invisible window," she said. "But it was interesting, unless I misunderstood, that these old items showed up after he turned it off."

Then, Marcum's landlord evicted him and he disappeared for a few months. According to a *New York Times* December 8, 1996, story, "In late September, Marcum vanished, and *The St. Joseph News-Press* chillingly reported that he'd been evicted from his apartment, allegedly for transporting a cat 'a block away.' Marcum resurfaced last month, taking umbrage with 'the cat deal—it just ain't true.' As for his gizmo, he plans to test it as soon as he solves the sticky problems of controlling when and where it sends him. 'Right now,' he said. 'This would only make a good garbage disposal.'"

During Marcum's second, and last, appearance on Bell's show in 1996, he said he was thirty days away from completing his "legal" time machine. By January 1997, Marcum had seemingly disappeared . . . and

Sanderson was worried about him. "Michael was a rather lost young man emotionally and he had a counselor appointed by the court when he got in trouble over the electrical transformers," she said. "Michael was rather private about his past and I got the impression that he didn't have a great childhood." Sanderson tried to keep in contact with Marcum; she sent Christmas cards but he didn't write back. "We never heard from him again. He had no phone or cell phone," Sanderson said. "I continue to wonder how he is and where he is."

The world of paranormal chat last heard from Marcum via a post on an Internet chat room discussing voltage, Jacob's ladders, and power arcs on December 15, 2003, at 8:01:46 p.m. In the post, he said he moved to Cincinnati a "few years ago." Sanderson describes Marcum as about 5'5" with blue or green eyes and red hair. "He was very slender and wiry," she said. "He was a quick-acting fellow and a deep thinker. He did not smile and was continually serious when we were with him. He did have a few buddies ... but most of the time, he was a loner."

But could his time machine actually work? Northwest Missouri State University physics professor Dr. Dave Richardson and chemistry and physics professor Dr. Rick Toomey both doubt Marcum's claims. "What he's basically produced is localized lightning," Richardson said. "It will produce heat but not enough in that localized area [to produce the anomalous circle Marcum claimed]." And, even so, if Marcum's machine worked, we'd have time vortexes everywhere. "Any phenomenon he could create with a transformer could be created with every lightning strike," Toomey said. So are there any current theories that use electricity in time travel? "Nothing," Richardson said. "Absolutely nothing."

According to physics, the main problem with Marcum's time machine is that it doesn't correspond with any current time-travel theory. "All the potential time travel involves gravitational effects and really high speeds," Richardson said. "There's really no theory that includes electricity and gravity together." Tying the two together, Toomey added, would be the Holy Grail of physics. Even if Marcum had done this, Toomey foresees other problems. "When you look at the equations I don't know if a biological system could maintain its integrity," he said. "I just can't imagine your nervous system can go through that and survive."

Marcum had the same concern. "If you can go through it without being killed you can use it as a time machine," Marcum told the *News-Press* in 1995. "With death a risk factor, I'm not ready to step into an electrically charged vortex. There's still some stuff I've got to iron out." Neither Richardson nor Toomey think time travel will be ironed out anytime soon. "Sure, we could wake up and time travel could be real," Toomey said. "[But] these discoveries are not going to happen in our lifetime. We'll all be long dead before that."

So, was Marcum sane or ... "Crazy?" Lupfer said. "No, he was smart. He wasn't a dumb guy. He just had this in his head and thought he could do it." And maybe Marcum was the right guy to try to build a time machine. "I was always considered sort of a mad scientist for stuff like making nitroglycerin in chemistry class," Marcum said in a 1995 interview in the *News-Press*. One of Marcum's jailers in 1995 wouldn't commit to Mike's success in time travel, but wouldn't deny it either. "Only Jules Verne knows that," the jailer said. Some people who've followed the Marcum story credited his disappearance to the fact that he actually invented a time machine.

Cincinnati resident Vince Parks said Marcum has made such a claim recently. "I know Mike Marcum," Parks said. "He lives less than ten miles from me to this day." Marcum moved into the 12th Street apartment complex in Cincinnati where Parks lived in 2006. Parks and Marcum would drink soda, play video games, and talk about time travel. "At that time he regaled me with stories of his attempts to create a time machine," Parks said. "I held with my own two hands a couple of the high voltage signs he stole along with those transformers in Missouri." And Parks, who holds a PhD in electrical engineering, was hooked. "It is actually possible he had a complete working device at one point, but I don't think he fully understood what he'd discovered." Marcum told Parks his whole story—the Jacob's ladder, items disappearing and reappearing "in a bright flash, according to him," Parks said.

Then, Marcum talked about his personal journey. "He did tell me a story of being foolhardy enough to actually walk into this himself," Parks said. "According to him, he was completely lost for a moment, and in a fit of bioelectric shock found himself back in the basement some hours later." During those missing hours, Marcum claimed to see the basic geography that surrounded his house [at the time] but in his journey there was no house. "He asked me what I thought that could mean, and I told him any number of things," Parks said. "It could be some time down the line, at a point where the structure had given to entropy, or some time before the structure was there." But there was something more to Marcum's stories of time travel that made Parks take him seriously. "The two things that throw me," Parks continued, "he discussed at one point how cool certain video game concepts would be, in very good detail, and I seem to recall almost a year later, early Internet articles on those very games starting to emerge. Now of course that could be coincidental, but he hit home on seven games I can think of." Games like an installment in the Final Fantasy series that had been kept secret until the game was launched. "Also, a first-person shooter called Bioshock... a very right-on description of Super Mario Galaxy, which was also kept pretty tight. What else? Ah yes, Assassin's Creed." Parks said Marcum didn't mention the titles of these games; he just described them as if he'd played them. Marcum also described to Parks a much-touted Apple product. "One that somewhat threw me was his talking about how cool a PC in a phone would be," Parks said. "He described what sounded just like the iPhone." Marcum talked about this two years before the iPhone was released.

Later, Marcum told Parks of his further travels in time. Marcum told Parks that the Earth will be "an improved place, cleaner, less dingy... a smell of new, if you will. But he did kind of hint that this new place was built on the smoldering ruins of what was." Parks said Marcum believes he went two hundred and fifty to three hundred years into the future. "Sadly, and he made a point to point this out, no flying cars," Parks said. "He did say he believed the vehicles mostly drove themselves, which I find wholly believable." As for physical artifacts, Marcum showed Parks items he claimed to have brought from the future. "I have worked with all manner of tool and technology in this world, and two things he had were unlike things I have seen," Parks said. "At first surmise, I believed he fabricated them, but they were too machine-polished for homebrew." One item was a central processing unit Parks said was from "a brand new field of CPU architecture that is nowhere near that level," he said. "We're nowhere near building an FPGA [a semi-conductor: field-programmable gate array] with that density and with such small run pins. The pins were human-hair size."

Although Parks has not seen Marcum since 2006, he gave a description quite similar to Sanderson's: "He's an amicable geek," Parks said. "He tends to stick largely to himself, generally associating only with other geeks or machine heads primarily. He is an avid video game nut, primarily into role-playing games such as the Final Fantasy series." But since 1997, Marcum seems to be finished with public life and with that goes interviews. He lives alone, Parks said, and lives off disability, "because the government thinks he's nuts." But he's also continuing his work on time travel. "To this day he's still trying," Parks said. "And yeah, he's not nuts. He's pretty clever, just odd."

7

The Possession of Travis White

A shadow lurked in the room of eleven-year-old Travis White. The black human shape leaned in from the folds of night that filled the edges of Travis's room as he lay trapped under his covers—terrified. "I've seen them a lot," Travis, now twenty-two, said, "the shadows." The shadow figure moved the first night he saw it, crisscrossing the floor where, during the day, Travis played in the sunlight. "He was zigzagging across the room," Travis said. "I didn't really see him walk, and then he was at the end of my bed." As the darker-than-night figure, draped in a cloak, stood over Travis, the boy screamed and leapt for the light switch. As the light shot on the entity changed. "It seemed like it turned red and it was gone … poof," Travis said. Travis's father, Brandon, rushed into the room, but found only his shaking son. The entity may have gone, but it hadn't gone far—it somehow attached itself to Travis.

Brandon said Travis's troubles started, in part, because of the house. "There was a lot of activity when he started seeing it when we were at Fairfax," Brandon said. Their home near Fairfax—population 645—was a Victorian mansion that was the center of the old family farm, a house where Brandon had once been lifted off his bed and cast to the floor by a black, birdlike shadow. And, what Brandon feels is the focal point of what was to come, the family wasn't religious. "As is not uncommon, a lot of times it stirs things up a little bit," Brandon said. "None of us had been Christians yet, so it opened us up to the darker side of things." At night, the ghost of Brandon's uncle would often visit Brandon's younger son, Garrett. An unexplained will-o'-

the-wisp began to appear outside the house and wander off through the outbuildings when followed, and a black orb appeared—but only once. "One week there were a series of events, starting with—picture this—a small, black orb with lots of flashing lights on it. Like the ball Luke Skywalker trained with, but black," Brandon said. "One night this floated into our bedroom. We got up and chased it into the hallway. It goes behind an old mirror. There's a doorway kind of closed off back there. We never saw where it went." The next night, Travis saw the shadow figure in his room—a figure he wouldn't see again until he was a senior in high school.

That year, something strange was in Travis's head. A sensation dragged Travis, at the time seventeen, from sleep. As he struggled to pull open his eyes, he found he wasn't alone. The shadow figure was back, but it was different—it was just a face. "I would wake up and feel weird," Travis said. "I'd wake up and there was this face." The face hovered at the edge of his vision, a distorted, fuzzy black shape, but after many nights of the face coming closer and closer into his field of vision, it gradually changed. The bolder it became, the clearer it appeared to him. "As I started seeing it more, I saw more detail," Travis said. "The face was humanoid, but scarred. It was dark red and obviously had a broken nose. When I first saw him, he was wearing a hood, but later I saw the face. I recognized it was what I saw as a kid."

But Travis wasn't the only one who saw entities in the house— his father saw shadows, too. "The first time [Travis saw it] it was a red figure. A deep red," Brandon said. "It was also the same time the dark figures started. I started seeing dark figures at that time." But as the entity crept ever deeper into Travis's life, Travis began to ignore it. Why not? He had a steady job, a girlfriend, and he was planning to go into the seminary. Things for Travis were good. Then the face began speaking to him and his life crashed into the dirt. "[Before] I started hearing his voice, I was probably the happiest I'd ever been," Travis said. That happiness didn't last.

Travis had ridden to church with a friend one Sunday morning in April 2006 when the face became too intrusive to ignore—it told him to leave the church. "I just ignored it," Travis said. "Then in my chest I get this terrible pain. My head hurt, I was sweating." Travis stood and staggered into the narthex and out to the sidewalk. "As soon as I was out it all went away," Travis said. "[The voice] was male and it was weird because I could tell I wasn't hearing it. I didn't hear a sound, but I could *hear* it. It was like you're thinking. I know I wasn't hearing a voice. It was coming from somewhere else." And it was angry—angry that Travis was in church. "It wasn't like, 'hey, get out, please,'" he continued. "It was … '*GET OUT*.'" As Travis stood on the sidewalk, the pain slowly fading from his head and chest, he had no time to think about what had just happened to him—the voice in his head spoke to him again. "After he told me to leave the church, I was standing outside the church and the voice told me to go home, so I [walked] home," he said. "It told me to get in the car, and three hours later I was in New Market by Platte City [Missouri]." Travis had driven seventy-six miles and remembered little of it. His family didn't know what had happened to him. "We had no idea where he went. He was just gone," Brandon said. "He was sitting with his friends and just got up and walked out. It was very strange." All Travis could recall from his drive were a few glimpses of scenery. "Then I came to this full awareness that I was at a gas station," he said.

Hours often began to disappear from Travis's day—always after the voice had spoken to him. "I've lost three hours a lot," he said. "As time went on after April it was once a week, then twice a week, then it was two to three times a day I'd hear or see him." And the face was changing, along with Travis's mood. "As time went on it got less angry and more friendly," Travis said. "As I grew dark in my personality— more depressed—it got more happy." Travis avoided sleep, a helpless state where the face began to rule over him, infecting his dreams. He avoided work because he didn't want to explain that he was talking to a voice in his head. He'd go into the parking lot for an hour of restless sleep in his car. And he avoided school because he was exhausted. "It got to the point where I did not sleep because I didn't want to dream about it," he said. "It played on all my insecurities and fears. He knew everything about me. He seemed to hate everything I enjoyed."

Then, in October 2006, Travis died. "I died from alcohol poisoning," Travis said. "I was dead for like a minute. The doctors brought me back. My dad said it was a gift from God. I started to think it was from somewhere else." Today, Brandon agrees with

Travis—his 'gift' may have been from somewhere dark. "His heart stopped twice and he stopped breathing five times," Brandon said. "During any of these, he could have crossed the path of something he shouldn't have. He wasn't at a good spot. With his dark emotions he could have attracted something." Time would often disappear from Travis's memory. "I will have a couple of hours here or there when I was just gone," he said. "Where I was, I have no idea."

As the face's power over Travis grew, Travis began to accept it. "For a while I was very depressed all the time," he said. "Once I got used to it, I didn't have that big of a problem. Part of it made me stronger. I was insecure. It played on those insecurities." Those insecurities included his relationships with his family, friends, and girlfriend. "He hated my [now] ex-girlfriend," Travis said. "He would disappear when I talked to her." But every time Travis saw her, talked to her on the telephone, or mentioned her in conversation, the face punished him. "I would suffer serious migraines," he said. "Dad would come out and find me face-first on the lawn." But the more Travis spoke about her—and his father—the more hate the voice spewed. To the point where the voice told Travis to kill them. "When the figure told Travis you need to kill your girlfriend, telling him to do bodily harm to someone, Travis started talking with me about it," Brandon said. "We started talking about how to protect yourself."

At this point, Travis knew if he was going to continue to live, the entity had to go. "I eventually told [Dad] everything because it kind of freaked me out," he said. "Dad said, 'We're going to get rid of it.' After that the voice told me not to talk to my dad." In September 2007, Travis and Brandon confronted the thing that controlled Travis. "I sat down with my dad and we prayed about it. He did the whole Baptist minister 'demon be gone' thing," Travis continued, slapping his forehead. Travis and Brandon sat in their home and prayed—prayed for the entity to be gone. "[Travis] was very frightened," Brandon said. "We just prayed with him right there. We said, 'You're not welcome in this house. Leave him alone. He can evoke the name of Christ any time he wants. If you want to take the gloves off and [have us] bring someone in here who can get rid of you, we'll do it.'" Then the face began to fade. "A couple of days later [the face had] gotten less and less frequent," Travis said. "He's either gone or I just can't hear him." Although Brandon now sees shadow figures in his family's new home in Maryville, Missouri, he is convinced that he and Travis banished the entity. "I think we did successfully ban it from the house," Brandon said. "We kicked it out of the house out at Fairfax. We banned it through the protection of Christ, so it wasn't a good guy."

Exorcist James D. Bucknam of Beverly, Massachusetts, said Travis sounds like the victim of partial possession. "The entity in question would manipulate [Travis] to cause him to be destructive to himself and others," Bucknam said. "It would be a wearing-down process until [Travis] gives up and gives himself completely to the invading entity." Bucknam said Brandon and Travis did the right thing by praying and ordering the entity out of Travis's life. "The fact that the son fought back speaks well in his favor," Bucknam said. "The prayers he and his father did made the energy around the son more uncomfortable for the entity to be near him. It makes sense to me that the entity would back off at this point." But Bucknam offered a dire warning about demonic energies such as the one that preyed on Travis. "Unfortunately, many times this type of entity does not go away, it simply retreats into the background," he warned. "Just because things are quiet now doesn't mean this entity has completely gone away."

Although the face has grown distant, Travis occasionally feels its presence when he sleeps. "As of right now, he's gone," Travis said. "Except my dreams. I haven't seen him or had a conversation with him since September." Brandon, however, sees dangerous signs some-thing is still not right in his son's life. "Travis is depressed and having trouble in college," Brandon said. "I'm trying to convince him to go to the doctor about the depression. He can't go to sleep, can't wake up. He's broken. He needs [to be] fixed."

After Travis joined a fraternity during the spring 2008 semester, his grades suffered. Travis would routinely miss classes and missed most of that semester after midterm exams. "He's now moving into the frat house," Brandon said. "I don't see how that's going to help him. He's continuing to expose himself to lifestyles that aren't conducive to protecting himself. [The protection] started working when we started working with the ministry and went to church." Bucknam agrees—a negative lifestyle attracts negative forces. And once attached, negative forces don't like to let go. "All negative entities, especially demonic ones, are first and foremost a predator," Bucknam said. "Their main goal is to cause individuals to lose sight of who they are and weaken them. A demonic entity will feed off of your pain, and eventually make you their personal hand puppet. Like all predators, they won't come at you when you are in a position of strength. They will be very patient and wait for a moment of vulnerability, then they will start working the person again." This is what worries Brandon, that the negative entity will return. Although Brandon still sees fleeting shadows in the corner of his eye, Travis has placed his possession in the past. He has a job and a girlfriend, and considers what he went through to be over. "Part of me always thought it was an exorcist type of thing. Some kind of entity attached itself to me," Travis said. "I'm just glad it's gone. It was a painful year."

8

A Life I Never Lived

Cold, sterile light flooded the quiet, white operating room. An anesthesiologist fitted a mask over Della Hooper's nose and mouth and released a gas that she sucked into her lungs in even, cool breaths. Moments later, the room began to swim and unseen weights pulled Hooper's eyelids shut. She almost never opened them again.

"In 1984, I had a hysterectomy and died," Hooper, of Clarinda, said. "[At first] they couldn't revive me." As Hooper lay on the operating table, doctors and nurses working over her, something happened within her deeper than a scalpel can reach—something happened to her soul. The doctors eventually stroked her back to life, but when she later awoke in an anesthetic haze, they couldn't explain the symptoms she described to them. "My body was so sore," she said. "I felt like someone had taken a baseball bat and beat me with it. I said something to the doctor, 'why am I so sore?' The doctor said, 'I have no explanation for that.'"

Chris Brethwaite of Raytown, Missouri, runs the Kansas City chapter for the International Association for Near-Death Studies, and said this feeling is not common among people who have had a near-death experience. "I haven't heard of this," he said. "NDEers [Near-Death Experiencers] will frequently say that when they returned to their bodies they were once again in pain, but that's because they were in a painful situation to start with, usually as the result of disease or physical trauma." But Hooper found an explanation much, much later: while she was dead, her soul traveling out of her body, another spirit attached itself to her. "When you have a near-death experience and your soul leaves you, another one can come inside you," she said. She believes a spirit, something she calls a "walk-in," took hold of her

44

body when she died and literally changed her life. "After that, I was not the same person," she said. "It opened my mind." Hooper's "walk-in" brought to her a world of ghosts, alien abduction, past lives, and psychic ability.

Hooper's rural Iowa farmhouse seemed oddly out of place to Hooper when her family brought her home. The land, the trees, the house, the pictures, were as familiar as they were strange. She was home, but she wasn't. As she went through her once-normal daily routine, it seemed false—a charade. This farmwife and mother didn't understand why she changed the radio to music she'd never before enjoyed, nor why the food she chose for dinner was nothing she'd ever liked. Although Hooper had a near-death experience, Brethwaite said it is different than any others of which he has heard. "I've heard of people receiving organ transplants and suddenly finding themselves with different tastes in food, music, TV, etc., but it's not something you find in NDE accounts," he explained. "NDEers change in other ways, mainly because of the perceived truths they were exposed to on the other side. For example, they'll become more loving, caring, and altruistic. Additionally, they tend to become more spiritual and less religious. They also tend to show greater regard for the planet and the environment. Some will change their careers, usually to something that is more beneficial to humankind. However, their personal tastes tend to stay the same." All Hooper knew is that something had changed in her life—something drastic.

One day, as Hooper stood at a window looking out across the farm, she saw something move—it was a man. The old man, gray whiskers hiding his face, wore a floppy, sweat-stained hat, the brim working to keep the sun from his eyes. His clothing was from another century. As the old man walked slowly across Hooper's field of vision, with a pack mule laden with leather satchels trailing behind him, she realized that she knew him. He was a gold prospector, his name was Barnie, and he was dead. No one else in her family had seen the man and his mule. "Shortly after I got home I started seeing things," she said. "Before that, I had seen none of this." American Indians in native dress rode horses bareback across her Iowa farm as they had before white settlers had worked their way west. No one in her family could see the things that had begun to invade Hooper's world until she photographed something that made the unknown real.

A clear blue sky swept from horizon to horizon the day Hooper walked across the fields of the family farm and into the nearby timber, snapping pictures of flowers, insects, and wildlife. "The weather was perfect that day," she said. "Lavender flowers were blooming on the floor of the woods and the sky was clear; it was springtime." She wasn't alone in the timber, but she never once suspected this until the film she'd taken of wildflowers was developed. "I took a picture of two little beings about two feet tall wearing helmets," she said. "I took a picture of flowers and I didn't see the two little guys. If I'd have seen them there, I wouldn't have approached them—they didn't look friendly." When she got the prints back from the developer, she took them to a lab in nearby Creston, Iowa. "I got a better look at their faces," she said. "They were pixyish, but mean." But what surprised Hooper even more was she knew what they were doing. "I instantly thought they were gathering plants and soil samples," she said. Although she didn't know why she thought that at the time, she believes she found out soon after.

The farmhouse was asleep, her husband and children quiet as the night crawled by. But something began dragging Hooper into consciousness and she suddenly snapped awake—her body pinned to the bed, paralyzed. "I didn't know what was happening to me," Hooper said. "I was just a plain housewife. I didn't know anything about this. I'm in bed and I can't move and I can't breathe. Then, boom, I wasn't in bed anymore." The next moment she stood on a cold floor, a multiple-picture television screen dominating the room. "I was on a ship," she said—an alien ship. She was no longer paralyzed, and she was not alone. Hooper walked tentatively around the metal room, looking at foreign instruments and shapes, but was drawn to the screen. "There was Egyptian-like hieroglyphics on the equipment," she said. "There was a large ET [extraterrestrial] who watched me. He didn't touch me, he just watched me." Her guard was hairless with whitish-gray skin and large black eyes, and was much larger than the other similar-looking entities in the room. The many smaller entities ignored her as she explored their ship and watched scenes of war, floods, and political discussions from across the world flash across the television screen. "They were just sitting there watching what the world was doing," Hooper said. She woke up later in her bed. Brethwaite said those who have died and come back to life are more open to alien encounters. "Experiencers are more likely to believe in life on other planets than non-experiencers," Brethwaite said. "Again, this is because of information they were exposed to on the other side. Additionally, I have heard of NDE accounts that included traveling through space and seeing other planets and solar systems. Famed psychologist Carl Jung claimed that he saw the Earth from high above during an NDE he had in the late 1940s. Interestingly, his description of the Earth closely matched satellite photos taken decades later." But no one around Hooper—husband, children, family, or friends—took any of her experiences seriously. Then, suddenly, the opinions of her family and friends became less important.

Strange memories as real as her own started flooding her mind. Memories of mountains she'd never seen, faces she'd never looked upon, names she'd never known. Knowing no one would believe her or would try to understand what was happening to her, Hooper started writing these new memories in a journal. Cities, the names of people she'd known—like Barnie the prospector—geographic landmarks, and times she had traveled to them dashed from her pen until she'd written three-hundred pages of somebody else's life in Pine Valley, Colorado. Hooper had never been to Colorado, but the memories were real enough to prompt her to call directory assistance and ask to be connected to anyone in Pine Valley. "But Pine Valley, Colorado, doesn't exist anymore," Hooper discovered. However, the city, now known as Pine, does. Directory assistance connected her to the local grocery store. Hooper started asking about landmarks she'd never seen with her eyes and the women she spoke with said she was correct. The grocery store eventually connected Hooper with Pals Books, a bookstore in nearby Conifer, Colorado, and a door into a life she'd never had was thrown open.

Hooper drove to Colorado and visited the bookstore owner. "We turned out to be the best of friends," she said. "My marriage ended not long after that." Hooper moved to Colorado in 1986 to explore the past life of her "walk-in." She discovered everything she remembered was true, especially the geography. "The main thing that really got to me was I knew Colorado," she said. "I had always lived in Iowa, but I could drive right to where I knew things were." After a hypnotic regression session with a professional in Denver, Hooper was told that, yes, she was inhabited by a "walk-in" soul. This comforted Hooper. "It's made me a better person," she said. Her friend, the bookstore owner, "died some years ago," Hooper related. "I miss her every day."

Since Hooper moved back to Iowa from Colorado, she has used the psychic gifts given to her by her "walk-in"—like seeing ghosts—to help others, such as cleansing homes of negative spirits in Clarinda. "I've always been successful in doing that," she said. People also ask her to interpret dreams and advise them on the afterlife, but she has noticed these topics are more taboo in the Midwest. "In Colorado…the people were so open-minded with this, you could hear alien abduction stories and ghost stories in the grocery store like you're talking about buying a loaf of bread," she said. Things aren't like that for Hooper in Iowa. "My abilities bother some people," she said. "But [I don't] let that bother me. I don't push it on anybody. If someone has something paranormal and wants me to help, I will." However, she said many people aren't ready for the truth about the invisible world around them. "I think there's a lot out there we don't know," Hooper said. "There's a lot out there [that] if we did know, it would scare us to death."

9

Footprints in the Carpet

Marnie is the only one who lives in the one-level, four-bedroom house in Tarkio, Missouri, but she is never alone. At eighty-seven, Marnie has Alzheimer's disease, and it's the job of six women to care for her. Barb Murphy is one of these women and she is convinced Marnie's house is haunted. "I started working there about five years ago and I started noticing a few things that happened," Murphy said. "I thought it was just me. I thought I was going nuts."

Murphy has felt cold spots, smelled pipe tobacco smoke even though no one is allowed to smoke in the house, and witnessed lights come on although no one touched them. "There are several lights, like lamps in her bedroom, that nobody ever messes with," she said. "I went through the hallway, there was a light on in her bedroom that none of us ever, ever turn on." As she walked down the hallway to turn the light off, she felt it. "It felt cold that way," she said. "I felt someone was there. I felt the hair go up on the back of my neck. I didn't like being there." She often feels uncomfortable in the hallway that goes down the middle of the house, connecting the front rooms with the bedrooms. Murphy is convinced something is wrong there. "I don't like it. I don't like the feeling I get," she said. "I feel there's someone there watching me when I'm in the hallway. Some of the other girls don't like the hallway either." Standing in the kitchen folding laundry with her back to the hallway in March 2009, Murphy was engulfed with an overwhelming feeling. "I felt someone was standing right behind me," she said. "I turned around real slow and no one was there. It sure felt like someone was there."

But what really bothers her are the footprints. "I clean the house every Friday," she said. "In her living room, [Marnie] has a baby grand

49

Ghostly footprints walk under a chair and piano in this Tarkio, Missouri, home. Sometimes the mysterious footprints are found in a hall closet. (Photo courtesy of Barb Murphy)

piano. Right beside the piano she has two old Windsor chairs and a table. I was walking in there—I had just vacuumed—and there were footprints that went under the chair and under the piano and just disappeared. I thought I was seeing things." Murphy called another woman into the room to look at the prints; she saw them, too. "And she said, "Oh my God, they go underneath the piano,'" Murphy said. The footprints were long and narrow; too long and narrow to fit anyone who worked in the house. "They were bare feet," Murphy said. "You could see the toes. They went into a corner and they were gone." Two weeks later, it happened again. "I had vacuumed the hallway on Friday morning," Murphy said. "My boss called me that evening and asked, 'Did you happen to vacuum the hall?' I said, 'Yes.'" But there were footprints in the hall. "There's two little footprints that look like [child's] footprints, the size of a one- or two-year-old child." The prints looked as if they walked into the closet and didn't come out. "There haven't been any children at the house whatsoever," she said.

Although the strange occurrences in the house surprise Murphy, they don't frighten her. "I'm okay with this," she said. "I don't feel threatened in any way. When you feel the cold, it's more of a sad, strange feeling. But as soon as something touches me, I'm out of there."

10

Big Monkey in My Backyard

Legends of hairy ape-like creatures span centuries and the world. Wildmen stalked medieval European forests, the Alamas wanders the Caucusus of Russia, Yeti eludes climbers in the Himalayas, the Yowie lurks in remote forests and mountains of Australia, and Bigfoot or Sasquatch prowls the mountains of the Pacific Northwest in North America. For thousands of years, indigenous peoples have known and interacted with these creatures. People of the modern Western world have been slow recognizing them, but Missourian Ron Boles is different from most.

Boles encountered one of these hulking, hairy beasts in the late 1980s in southern Missouri (outside my 100-mile range). Since then, he has dedicated himself to researching an animal unrecognized by science. He is an investigator for the Bigfoot Field Researchers Organization (BFRO), a group using scientific research to investigate the mystery of Bigfoot. "The scientific community won't be happy until one is alive in a cage or dead on a slab," Boles said. "Our job is to research. We're not out to shoot one, to capture one or kill one. The idea of killing one absolutely mortifies me."

The BFRO estimates the Bigfoot population in the United States is between 6,000 and 10,000, although "we suspect there are more than 20,000," Boles said. According to those who are convinced Bigfoot exists, these creatures are a North American species of ape, usually six to ten feet tall, six hundred pounds, and nocturnal. "We think they're descendent of the *Gigantopithecus*," Boles said, referring to a ten-foot-tall species of Pleistocene ape indigenous to Asia. "They probably came

The entrance to Krug Park in St. Joseph, Missouri, home to Bigfoot sightings in the mid-1960s.

over with the mammoths and people on the land bridge [that connected Siberia to Alaska roughly 14,000 to 11,000 years ago]."

The animals, Boles said, are curious, but cautious. "These are very intelligent creatures," he explained. "A full-grown chimp has the intelligence of a five-year-old. A gorilla in captivity, Koko, uses sign language at the level of a twelve-year-old. Imagine the capacity of an even larger primate with a larger brain mass." Apart from plaster casts of the up to twenty-seven-inch footprints that give Bigfoot its name, Boles said the BFRO has scat, hair, and blood samples of the creature. However, this evidence has not been enough to convince mainstream scientists the creature exists.

Other native Missourians, such as Bill Bowen and Larry Lawhon, don't need convincing.

Logging camp just outside St. Joseph: 1932
Black walnut trees scatter the hills of Buchanan County in northwest

Missouri, sometimes sparsely, sometimes as thick as the day the county was settled. Something terrifying stepped out of these trees at a logging camp in 1932. A towering, hairy, gorilla-like creature walked into the camp on two feet and changed the lives of two young couples.

Bill Bowen, the son of one couple, Alta and Raymond Bowen, and nephew of the other, Frank and Lucy (Bowen) Goodpastor, heard the story of a Bigfoot encounter from his parents throughout his life. "When I was a young boy, just a child, I had four sisters," Bowen said. "Mom and Dad used to tell us this story. It was always the same. They would talk about this gorilla-looking creature that would come to the camp where they stayed."

The Bowens and Goodpastors arrived at the logging camp looking for work. The men were hired and the couples shared a cabin. The men left the women at home while they worked in the forest from dawn to dusk "hewing out railroad ties by hand," Bowen said. And after one hard week of work, the men wanted to relax. "My mother said one night the men got in from work," Bowen said. "It was Saturday night and they decided they all would go into town."

Lucy Goodpastor was a jealous woman; she fumed as she watched her husband drive away in the darkness towards town and, she worried, into the arms of another woman. Angry, Goodpastor sat on the porch waiting for her husband to come home. "She had her knees up and her head on her knees," Bowen said. "She was crying." Goodpastor felt something approaching and when she turned, she saw a giant, lumbering figure not two feet from her. She screamed and it ran. Goodpastor was the only person in the camp to see the creature that night. "Later, the men came home and she told the men what happened," Bowen said. "They made fun of her. Everybody thought she was just loony. It wasn't long before they all seen it, more than once."

The "thing," as they called it, would walk out of the woods at dusk and put its elbow on the bed of a logging truck (about six feet off the ground) and rest its chin in its hand and look at them. "Mom and Dad said it was bigger than a man and had hair all over its body," Bowen said. "They said it looked something like a gorilla. Dad said it looked a little like it didn't have a head, its head was down in its shoulders."

The creature would stand by the truck, about two hundred feet from the cabin, and stare at Bowen's family. The Bigfoot would run upright faster than the dogs chasing it. "Dad would say, 'Those dogs could chase down a rabbit but they couldn't keep up with that thing,'" Bowen said. Bowen's cousin was eleven years old at the time of the encounters and lived in the cabin, but never got to see the creature. "He said he was always somewhere else," Bowen said. "But he said his father ran it off of my dad's truck because it had sat on the back of the truck."

Some men in camp talked about shooting the "thing," but Raymond Bowen, soon to be a Baptist minister, protested. "My dad wouldn't let them because it looked too human," Bowen said. "In the face it was too human. He was very protective of people."

Bowen's parents told him the story for the first time when he was nine or ten. Growing up, he asked them to tell the story again and again—and it was the same. "He never changed his story," Bowen said of his father. "After my father died, I knew my mother wouldn't be long. I'd have her to tell it to my children and I wanted them to hear that story from my mother." His father died in 1985 and his mother died in 2004. "My mother and father had told me this story before I had heard of Bigfoot, Abominable Snowman, or Sasquatch and I don't believe they had heard of such neither."

St. Joseph's Krug Park: 1966
The girl's story sounded like bunk. Larry Lawhon and his buddies sat in the school lunchroom in St. Joseph listening to a pack of teenage girls chatter about something that had happened the past weekend in a nearby park, something the boys considered unbelievable. "It was in the spring of 1966 and I was a senior in high school," Lawhon said. "At school we heard a girl talking about her and her boyfriend and other couples seeing something in Krug Park." The girl said the young couples were either making out or walking in the romantic moonlight when her boyfriend decided to dart into the darkness. "She claims her boyfriend took off running along this gravel path," Lawhon said, probably to wait along the path and scare them as they approached. But when he turned around to see if his friends were following, he

The thick wooded area at the rear of Krug Park stretches toward the Missouri River and is the type of habitat Bigfoot researchers say is prime for the creature.

didn't see what was on the path ahead. "He turned around and his face was suddenly in a big mound of hair." The boy had run full speed into a living being, a hairy, upright, towering, human-like creature. And it stopped him cold. The boy looked up at the thing in the darkness and terror overwhelmed him. "It started to put its arms around him and he passed out," Lawhon said. The girlfriend found him lying in the gravel path, alone, and she claimed the teens drove him to the local hospital, a visit Lawhon tried to confirm, but could not.

Yeah, right, Lawhon and his friends thought. It was probably just a joke. The boys had never heard the word Bigfoot and, even if they had, Lawhon doesn't think they'd have considered the girl's story a Bigfoot encounter. They thought it was mischief. "Me and some of my friends thought it was some kids trying to scare some other kids and that didn't set well with us," he said. Lawhon and five other seniors drove to the park the next weekend seeking the truth.

Krug Park was heavily wooded in 1966. It sits in the northwest side of St. Joseph, but at the time only a few farmhouses were nestled among its hills and river bluffs. Roy's Branch Creek runs nearby, traveling about a mile from Krug Park to empty into the Missouri River. Lawhon and five of his friends drove to the park the back way and stopped near a large open hillside near an abandoned rock quarry. They came prepared with walkie-talkies and brass whistles they used in ROTC. The boys broke up into two groups of three and started walking the park. It was a warm spring night and strong moonlight painted the darkness gray. One group went down to the creek; Lawhon's went up the hill. "We were walking along," Lawhon said. "I looked up ahead of me, and fifty feet away, a big, dark object moved across the roadway in front of me. I thought, 'I can't believe this; this thing is tall.'" Lawhon estimated the two-legged figure was at least seven feet tall, "maybe more," he said. "The roadway was ten to twelve foot wide and this sucker made it across the roadway in two strides." The creature was standing upright. "No stooped shoulders or anything," he said. "It didn't seem to be swinging its arms, either." Lawhon blew his whistle, the signal for the other group to turn on their radios. "Whatever it was it was taking some big strides," he said. "When I blew the whistle and took off running, it was gone. I was moving fast and this thing outdistanced me big time." As Lawhon chased after the creature, the other group arrived. "We came up the trail and a footpath took off into the timber," he said. "It was dark as pitch." Whatever Lawhon had seen was gone, but the boys found something it left behind. "It looked like one smeared footprint," Lawhon said, and it was big. "We'd had rain two or three days previous. It looked like a foot had hit this soft earth and made a smear." They'd seen enough. "Here we are, six fairly burly seniors in high school," he said. "We looked down the path and weren't going any farther. It was spooky."

The others in Lawhon's group didn't see the creature, but Lawhon wasn't the only eyewitness. "The three that were down by the creek said that before they heard me blow that whistle they were looking up and saw this," he said. "One of them was just getting ready to say, 'hey, there was something up there.'" After spotting the footprint, the boys ran to their car and sped back to Lawhon's house and their adopted clubhouse in the basement. "We went in there and stared at each other for a while," he said. "We were just plain baffled. At this time this topic [of Bigfoot] had never been brought up. We were just at a total loss. We just thought it was some person trying to scare the kids. We saw this thing and, uh-uh, this isn't a person."

Lawhon and his friends went back days later and couldn't locate the footprint. "To the best of my knowledge it was never sighted again," he said. "This one never made the news. Never made the paper. Nothing on TV or anything." But the encounter sparked an interest in Lawhon. "I ordered a book from [legendary Bigfoot researcher] John Green and sent a letter telling this encounter," he said. "I got a letter back stating, 'I wish I'd have gotten this before my book went to press because it would have been in it. From what I read, that's what you saw.' I treated that letter like it was the Declaration of Independence." Green's book was just the first of many books about Bigfoot Lawhon has read over the years, trying to learn more about the thing he saw as a high school senior on a moonlit night four decades ago. "This has stuck with me all these years," Lawhon said. "I can almost close my eyes and see that thing walking across the roadway."

11

The Axe Murder House

The people of Villisca wave when you're in their town. The yellow, industrial plastic playground equipment in the square's tree-lined center park looks strangely out of place among the old brick buildings and fading paint lining its surrounding streets, but the people are friendly and still do business in the old buildings. Bank Iowa, Country Love Antiques, DD Bar and Grill, and a drug store—Stoner Drug— surround the park. A young man sitting on a park bench waves at the cars that honk as they pass, while eating a sandwich for lunch. That's just how things work in the Midwest; things are quiet and peaceful, the sky is blue, and people wave at strangers.

But Villisca wasn't always so peaceful. In 1912, an unknown assailant with an axe killed the six-member Moore family and two children who were staying the night. The event crushed the spirit of that 1912 town and the murders have never been solved. The Olson Linn Museum at 323 East Fourth Street (a few blocks away from the murder house) is owned by Darwin Linn and his wife, Martha, who keep the memory of that incident alive. They bought the murder house in 1994 to preserve a piece of Villisca's history, and quickly found out that just because the Moore family has been dead for almost one hundred years doesn't mean they ever left home.

Darwin stood on the sidewalk in front of the museum on the southeast corner of the square, an old industrial fan roaring inside the storefront trying to ward off the heat of an Iowa July. Darwin, his head framed by a shock of white hair, smiled, showing a row of silver teeth, and nodded before sitting on a short wall, its fading white paint cracked and peeling. Darwin knows that ghost hunters, psychics, and curious onlookers are convinced his murder house is haunted. "This

A man with an axe slaughtered eight people in this Villisca, Iowa, home in 1912. Many people believe their ghosts—as well as the killer's—are still there.

year the numbers have risen right through the roof," he said. "For some, a cold breeze makes their night. The more people have hunted, [the more they] appreciate the small things that happen; it's the amateurs who expect something big. But I haven't had anyone ask for their money back. The only negative is when nothing happens." And, although he thinks the house might be haunted, he has not experienced anything strange there. "I haven't been pushed or my hair hasn't been pulled," Darwin said.

A cell phone clipped to the pocket of Darwin's bib overalls seemed a bit out of place in this Rockwellian setting. Sure, this town has a convenience store that makes pizza to order and there's a spot that rents DVDs, but everything else was like Beaver Cleaver's Mayfield, Ohio. "I didn't even know what a paranormal investigator was when one called in 1998," Darwin said. "I told him to come down and look at the house; I wasn't going to be around." Darwin and Martha both thought the investigator visiting (they don't live in the murder house) would be "kinda fun," but Darwin didn't foresee the circus he was bringing to the house. "I told everyone in the county," Darwin said. "I even put an ad in the paper telling he was coming." The night the paranormal investigator came, seventy to eighty people sat the yard. "They brought lawn chairs," Darwin said. "They were just curious." Curious to see if the white house, small for a two-story, still held some of the tragedy that brought national attention to Villisca five years before the United States entered World War I. Curious to see if the spirits of the people murdered in that home still stirred. The investigator eventually gave all the onlookers a tour of the house so they'd go home. They did, and the investigator spent the night there—more would follow.

The last time the people of Villisca saw the Moore family alive was at the annual Presbyterian Church Children's Day, on June 9, 1912. That night, the children of J. B. and Sarah Moore invited friends Lena and Ina Stillinger to stay the night. They all walked to the Moore home from the Presbyterian Church at 9:30 p.m. and were never again seen alive. A neighbor, Mary Peckham, went out to hang laundry on the line at 5:00 a.m. on June 10. Two hours later, she noticed no one had stirred from the Moore home. Around 8:00 a.m. she knocked on the Moore's door; no one answered and the door was locked. J. B.'s brother Ross eventually unlocked the door and found the carnage. J. B. Moore, forty-three, Sarah Moore, forty-four, Herman Moore, eleven, Katherine Moore, nine, Boyd Moore, seven, Paul Moore, five, and Lena and Ina Stillinger, lay in their beds, their skulls crushed. Mrs. Stillinger called to talk with her daughters that morning, but the operator told her no one would answer at the Moore house because everyone there had been murdered during the night. That was how Mrs. Stillinger learned that her children were dead. A number of people were suspects, from a drifter to a traveling preacher to a business rival of J. B. Moore's, but none were convicted of the murders. Is that why people feel the spirits of the victims remain in the house—to one day see their killer brought to justice?

Cindy Howard gives tours at the axe murder house, and she knows that the Moore and Stillinger children are there. "I just took a group on a tour yesterday from Omaha," she said on July 9, 2007. "I ended up giving the tour outside." Cindy had taken the tour to the second floor when something hit her. "All of a sudden, I couldn't breathe," she said. A closet in J. B. and Sarah's room leads to the attic door—the closet and attic doors were open. The attic, Darwin says, is important to the murder case. "[Federal officer M. W. McClaughry] speculated the killers hid there in the attic," he said. "There were spent cigarette butts there." As Cindy gasped for air, one of the people on the tour shut the attic door and Cindy's breathing returned to normal. "When the closet door's open I don't breathe very good," she said. People have long had problems with the closet and attic doors, Cindy said. The doors won't open for some people, and for others, they have a surprise. "This lady turned three sheets of white," Cindy reported. "They opened up the closet door and they could see a shadow going under the door like someone was pacing and one said they could feel someone on the other side holding the door shut. Then we booked it outside." At other times, Cindy has heard the attic door opening and slamming shut, but never went to investigate.

Others have also experienced the power of the attic. Janet Arnold and Jennifer Sparks of the ghost-hunting group Spirit Chasin' Ladies of Kearney, Missouri, have visited the axe murder house several times and have seen the door open and close. "When Michelle [Daley, another member of the group] and I were there last year, we were asking a lot of questions and the attic door opened and closed a few times," Jennifer said. "We didn't go into the attic. I don't like what I feel; I truly feel the killer is in the attic." Jennifer also refers to the killer as the bad entity. "That night we started off asking questions and the atmosphere changed," she said. "It started off being a normal conversation and it ended up being heavy, like you were being watched." Janet has also felt this bad entity. "When we go in the house, I feel something evil," Janet said. "I feel an evil presence." Darwin's nephew, Jeff Brown of Maryville, Missouri, has spent a lot of time in the house, from helping Darwin restore it to its 1912 state, to spending nights there with ghost hunters. He has witnessed contact with this bad entity. One night a ghost hunter lifted a sheet off the mirror in J. B. and Sarah's bedroom and saw something horrible. "All of a sudden he fell back and sat down on the bed," Jeff said. "He said, 'That's not the father, that's somebody else.' There's a large entity that roams around the house." There was a sheet over the mirror, because that's the way the house was found after the murders—all the mirrors had been covered, presumably by the killer.

The attic room where law enforcement authorities in 1912 believe the killer hid, waiting for the Moore family to return from a church picnic.

Psychics and children also sense the presence of spirits in the murder house. On the night the first ghost investigator gave towns-people tours of the house, Darwin saw these incidents firsthand. "A lady with a little girl came in and [the little girl] wanted to go in the other room," Darwin said. "It was dark there. This little boy did the same thing. He wanted to go in that room. I asked a psychic across the table from me and she said children are more open and they see kids in there and just want to play." Darwin looked into the room, and saw the children playing with something he could not see. "I began thinking maybe there is something in the house," he said. Jeff has also reported seeing children frolicking with invisible playmates, and Jennifer's group has even felt them. "One of the girls, she's real sensitive, she was sitting in a chair and something touched the back of her neck," she said. "I have it on film. You can see her reaction to being touched. It was like a child who liked to play with her hair. I definitely think the children are the most prevalent entities in the house."

The trip from the museum to the axe murder house at 508 East Second Street is short and the house is easy to find, a big sign with blood-dripping letters declaring from the front porch—The Villisca Axe Murder House: June 10, 1912. The day after the murders, hardware stores in town sold out of locks and weapons as the townspeople hoarded to protect their families from someone unknown and deadly. Before that, people in Villisca left their doors and windows unlocked. The Moore's windows weren't locked the night of the murders, but Darwin said spiderwebs and dust weren't disturbed from the windows—the killer, or killers, didn't break in. "There was no breaking and entering. J. B's wallet, money, and watch were left on the table," Darwin said. "The only thing they took from the house was the people's lives." The house was once out of town. Now, although on the outskirts of Villisca, it is surrounded by homes, not farmland. The white paint and gray-shingled roof make the house look like many others on the block—calm and quiet, although the attic windows, resembling the ones in *The Amityville Horror*, make the façade look ominous.

Darwin and Martha have tried to restore the house to its original state, even foregoing electricity. After the renovation, they successfully added the house to the National Register of Historic Places in 1997. Jeff volunteered to help with the work, but he didn't realize he was also volunteering to work with the dead. "When they bought the house I spent a lot of time up there helping them restore it," he said. "My first experience I really didn't recognize." Jeff was working in the Blue Room; he had just finished painting the room and was stenciling the border when something happened. "It was late June or early July and it was really warm," he said. "It was about dusk. I was up on a six-foot ladder and it got really cold in that corner where I was working and it felt like something was tugging on my pant leg. I could feel the hair go up on the back of my neck." He finished quickly and went home. Soon after, more paranormal investigators visited the house, and Jeff went back. "I went up to the house when they got there because I was curious," he said. The group set up monitors in the kitchen, running the electricity from a barn in the backyard. When night settled around them, the group sent a psychic through the house. "I was watching on the monitors," Jeff said. "It was dark, but with the infrared light you could see on the monitors." In the Blue Room, the psychic stopped on the spot where Jeff had felt the tug, and said, "There's an entity here." Jeff went into the room with the psychic and the area where he had worked was cold. "I said, 'What's that?' And he said, 'That's a ghost.' That's the first time I realized what had happened."

Downstairs in the house, pictures of the family glare from the walls, and toys and coins are scattered across the period furniture. Visitors bring modern toys for the spirits of the children, and others leave coins that are reported to fall to the floor for no apparent reason. It was in the Blue Room where the visiting children, Lena and Ina Stillinger, had slept that Jeff felt the entity. "Ina had taken a blow to the arm," Darwin said. "Many people think she saw the killer." When Ross entered the house that morning, he found something else strange in the Blue Room. "Killers took bacon out of [the] ice box," Darwin said. "They left part of the bacon on the piano and part on the bed in the Blue Room." Darwin speculates the killer, or killers, rubbed it on their feet to throw off the bloodhounds.

The staircase to J. B. and Sarah Moore's room, its rubber traction pads worn thin from years of visitors, is narrow. This is the room where the parents were murdered—the room that also leads to the attic. "J. B. was the only one killed with the sharp edge of the axe," Darwin said. "Everyone else was killed with the blunt side. They even used the Moores' axe. They took it out of the coal shed." The ceiling, long since repaired, was once scarred from the upswing of the axe as it fell again and again on the Moores. From those marks, federal officer M. W. McClaughry said the killer was left-handed. Two of the suspects were left-handed. The Moore children were sleeping in the room next to their parents. "The axe blows went straight up and down," Darwin said. "McClaughry said the trajectory proves the children were awake." Then there's the attic. A small white door set in the back wall of J. B. and Sarah's closet is lined with cracked plaster, a few old boards showing through. The area near the latch is dark with oil and dirt from hundreds, if not thousands, of strange hands. Through the small doorway in July is a warm, dusty attic, where a few flies buzz through the air and dead ones litter the floor.

Back downstairs, Darwin held a crystal. A multifaceted glass ball on a string hung on a pedestal on a table in the front room. Psychics carrying glass balls like these had visited the house, and had convinced Darwin they had used these glass balls to speak with Sarah. "I had two ladies from Lincoln, Nebraska, come," Darwin said. "They had glass crystals and they said it drew them to the entities." Darwin smiled. "I said, 'That's fine. I never paid too much attention to them.'" The women walked through the house, the glass balls swinging from side to side from their hands as they tried to speak with members of the Moore family. Then the women left, but Darwin heard from them again. "One night I left an axe in the house," he said, then one of the women called. "She said, 'Sarah didn't like that.' She'd call once every two months to tell me something Sarah didn't like." One year, box elder bugs were prominent in Villisca, and many had died on the living room floor of the axe murder house. "I moved the furniture to the center of the room and swept the bugs and left the furniture there," Darwin said. "And she sent an e-mail that night and said Sarah didn't like how I left the front room, and it made the hair on the back of my neck stand up. There's no way she could have known." Darwin lifted the crystal off the stand, held it by the string and spoke into the room. "Are you here Sarah?" he asked. "Is J. B. here? Are you happy here?" The glass ball swung on the string. "Sarah, can you tell us who your killer was?" he asked, but the glass stopped moving. "She never answers that question," Darwin said. Was Sarah talking to him? His face was stone. "I think so," he said. "I know in my own mind I'm not moving it."

The back door, maybe the same door a killer once walked through, is often open at the murder house; Darwin sees a lot of the same people. "Some who've been here many times, we go 'Here,' and leave them and have them shut the door," Darwin said. Ghost hunters occasionally stay on the property Friday and Saturday nights. Not in the house, but in a barn Darwin built in the backyard—complete with bathroom, microwave oven, and refrigerator—specifically for the ghost hunters. "They don't sleep very much," Darwin said. "They set their cameras up and sound equipment and leave the house to see what happens. Then they go out to the barn."

Nobody wants to stay in the Villisca Axe Murder House.

12

Entity in the Fire

The two-story white house was typical of old homes in small, midwestern towns. It was big: four bedrooms upstairs and two down, a large living room, a kitchen in the back, and a spacious front porch trimmed by partial brick pillars and shaded by large trees for lazy summer evenings. Martha Shireman moved into the house in 1988 with her daughter's family and later lived there with only her mother-in-law. The house had one famous resident. The late James Thomas Blair Jr., Missouri governor from 1957 to 1961, was born in the house. Soon after Shireman moved in, she realized something uninvited was in her home—it was an entity bathed in fire.

The first year in the home, Shireman's granddaughter saw someone walking around in the night. "She saw a person," Shireman said. "And she thought it was her uncle. She called him Duck." The six-year-old girl told Shireman the next morning that her uncle had been in the house, but Shireman didn't believe her. "I said, 'No. Your uncle's in [nearby] Cameron,' and she said, 'Well, I saw him.'" Soon after, Shireman began experiencing strange things in the house, too. Lights came on by themselves. Shireman often heard footsteps upstairs when no one was home, and small things disappeared only to reappear later. "One day I took the cap off a Pepsi bottle, laid it down on the counter, poured everybody's drinks, went back to put the lid on the bottle and it was gone," she said. "About three hours later I went back in and the lid was there again, right where I left it." Not long after Shireman's granddaughter saw someone walking around the house, she mentioned to people in the community that her house might be haunted. "A woman at the Senior Center said, 'Yeah. We've heard that house was haunted.'"

A spectral entity looms out the upstairs window of this Maysville, Missouri, home while it burned in 2005. (Photo courtesy of Martha Shireman)

Initially, only small things—like pictures falling from the walls—happened in Shireman's house. Then she heard voices. "I kept hearing my name called a lot," she said. "I had my mother-in-law staying with me, so I thought it was her." But, in the dark hours, when Shireman and her mother-in-law were alone in the old house, her name would creep to her through the darkness. "I'd hear my name," she said. "I'd go down to her room and she'd be sound asleep. I don't know if it was her talking in her sleep or the spirits." Shireman's mother-in-law never heard these voices or experienced the events Shireman did, but what happened one night convinced her that her daughter-in-law was not crazy. "My mother-in-law one night—she didn't believe in the ghost—she woke up in the middle of the night and every light in her bedroom was turned on, and she knows they were off when she went to bed."

Fire had damaged the house years before Shireman moved there. "I was told there was a fire in the kitchen and they rebuilt it," she said; that was the only reason she could explain the smell. "Anywhere in the house I'd smell smoke, and I'd go through the house looking for the source, and I never found it. I smelled smoke quite frequently in the kitchen." Fire struck again in 2005. The house didn't burn to the ground, but it was essentially destroyed. While Shireman and her family were salvaging what they could, Shireman made an odd discovery. "We went back inside the house and I found a frying pan at the top of the stairs," she said. "I never had any cooking utensils upstairs and I never had any stored in the attic either." Shireman blames the strange placement of the pan on whatever haunted her house.

A photograph of Shireman's burning house taken by a local insurance agent shows human-shaped figures looming in the flames that pour from the windows. From an upstairs window, a figure with outstretched arms and fiery orange eyes screams from a twisted, gaping mouth—maybe the same mouth that called Shireman's name.

13

A Haunted City

Brick streets line downtown Atchison, crawling up and down the hills of the bluffs of this Missouri River town. Long before the town existed, the Lewis and Clark expedition stopped on this spot in 1804 and celebrated the first Independence Day in the American West. The town, which in 1854 was named for Missouri Senator David Rice Atchison, became a popular spot for steamboat and westbound wagon traffic. Decades later when railroad lines stretched across America, Atchison became a hub for the Atchison, Topeka & Santa Fe Railroad. Because of the wealth brought by the railroad, Atchison is littered with grand old houses and mansions that peek from behind the trees covering the town. Three Kansas governors came from Atchison, but the town's most famous resident was aviator Amelia Earhart.

But Atchison's history has left more than just a legacy of the railroad, the river, and the American West. Atchison has been called the most haunted city in Kansas. The town embraces the claim, offering tours of haunted mansions, parks, and private homes where something—unlike the travelers that made this town grow—will not leave. "This town is known to have the most ghosts in the state of Kansas," said Ruth Stein of Atchison's Evah C. Cray Historical Home Museum. "Every place seems to have its own story."

Molly's Hollow
Jackson Park, on South Sixth Street, rolls across hills shaded by thick groves of trees. At the highest point in the park, parents watch from benches as their children frolic in the sand-lined playground. But at the lowest point in the park, where the day is just a little dimmer and the noise a little muffled, lurks a legend—the ghost of Molly's Hollow.

The ghost of a woman allegedly killed over love gone wrong in Atchison's Jackson Park screams at young lovers from the lowest area of the park.

The stories about Molly's Hollow differ. In one, a lynch mob hanged a young African-American woman in the park when they discovered she was having an affair with her white employer. In another, on the night of a school dance, a young man left his girlfriend in the park after they had an argument. The next day, people searching for the girl found her hanging from a tree in the park, her clothes torn and bloody. In a third, the couple was walking home when the young man broke off the relationship. The young woman walked away from the boy, climbed up Piano Rock Ledge, and jumped to her death.

Sally Webb, tourism coordinator for the Atchison Area Chamber of Commerce and Visitor Center, has investigated the legend and knows what really happened. "The one where she jumped is a true story," Webb said. "I've confirmed that with some of the people who are ninety years old in Atchison." But whatever story people hear, the story of the haunting is the same. Near midnight, if you scream into the hollow, the ghost of a young woman will scream back. "When you're there on the right night [at] the right time, you will hear Molly screaming as she jumps to her death," Webb said.

She should know—she's heard the scream. "I have," she said. "When I was high school age." Much like one of the stories about

Molly, a dance date took Webb home through the park. "He decided to show me Jackson Park, which was a lover's parking place," she said. "He said, 'Let's go see if we can hear Molly scream.'" Her date pulled into the hollow, stopped the car and told her to scream out the window. Webb laughed nervously as she rolled down the car window, then she screamed into the darkness. That night she met Molly. "A blood-curdling scream came back," she said. "It was not an echo. Needless to say, his plans came to an end. We went home."

Others haven't been so ... lucky?

Lysa Fris, founder of Fris Paranormal Investigations, was disappointed with Molly's Hollow. Bats danced under the dark gray clouds that slowly gathered over Atchison as Fris' group sat in the hollow, waiting for something to happen. Nothing did. "We spent some time there, approximately two hours," she said. "We decided that since we had been there long enough without any experiences or screams, we left." Before they drove to the bed and breakfast where they were to spend the night, the group went through the video and audio they recorded in the hollow. "I went through all of the pics from Molly's Hollow and unfortunately there was nothing," Fris said. "The audio and video proved to be nothing either. I can't say for 100 percent that the story is probably an old tale to spook the young ones, but that would be my guess."

There are historic elements to Fris's guess. Before Jackson Park was a park, it was the home of a man named Marlow who lived in a house in the hollow that bears Molly's name. While he lived there, the people of Atchison called the area Marlow's Hollow, and Webb said this was probably the origin of the modern name. "We are not even positive that Molly was what her name was," Webb said. The spot where Webb heard the scream bite through the night is easy to find. It's the lowest area in the park. The lane through the park winds over hills and thick trees, allowing slim glimpses of the hollow that has been a part of Atchison history for at least a century. "This is a very, very old haunted story. It's like folklore," Webb said. "My mother is eighty-nine years old and she heard it as a child. All of her friends knew of it. It's been handed down for a long time."

Sallie House

The little brick house at 508 North Second Street sits low to the ground, its foundation settling some since Michael C. Finney built it in 1867. The once-red bricks are painted white, the window trim is gray. A porch, whose roof is supported by two brick pillars, sits beneath one great second-floor window that stares out onto the street. Passersby might want to avoid looking at that window—who knows what might be looking back at them from behind the glass.

The house has had its share of tragedy. Michael C. Finney died in the house at ten o'clock at night on September 27, 1872, the first of three deaths in the house; the last was Agnes Finney, who died there at midnight on November 28, 1939. Others associated with the house have suffered worse fates. Johanna Barnes, a neighbor whose ghost is connected with the house, was judged insane in a court of law in 1887. According to a report in *The Atchison Globe*, Barnes was to "be taken from her home at that place to the asylum at Topeka in a wagon, and under the escort of a guard of four men. She has become so violent that nothing can be done with her save when her arms are tied behind her, and then it requires a crowd to do anything with her." After being

Something dark haunts the basement of this small Atchison home—so dark, according to investigators, that other spirits in the house are afraid of it.

released from the asylum and labeled "cured," she killed her six-year-old son, Frank, and tried to kill herself by turning on the gas in her apartment in Kansas City, Missouri, and lying down to sleep.

What could have caused this young woman's insanity? Could it have been something in the house? Something that is still there, lurking in the depths of the dark, quiet basement? Paranormal researchers who have investigated the house believe this is so.

Renae Leiker of Topeka, Kansas, has been involved with Sallie House investigations for more than six years, and she is convinced the house is haunted. Nails have dropped on her during investigations—old, handcrafted nails. "It was like a paper clip or something hitting you," she said. "Nothing was being worked on, or [there wasn't] an exposed ceiling. No explanation." Then there was the penny. During an investigation, an explosive boom shook up Leiker's group. "We went downstairs to try to find out what it was," she said. "And once we got downstairs someone looked down and found a penny. An 1862 Victorian penny. It was right in the middle of the floor. Many times we go in and vacuum the house to make sure there isn't anything like that because there are other groups that come in. It was definitely right in the middle of the floor where we'd been walking hours before."

Leiker has also experienced the typical traits of a haunting in the house: orbs, objects that inexplicably move from one place to the other, and strange noises. Brenda Marble's group, Miller's Paranormal Research, investigated the Sallie House in 2006, and found moving objects to be the most common—like Ping-Pong balls that rolled up an inclined floor and a teddy bear that fell off a window sill. "We have a lot of movement of items that we haven't experienced anywhere else," she said. "We've done close to one hundred investigations and you're very lucky to get one item that's moved. We've never experienced that many items moving. That way, it makes the Sallie House unique to us."

But the atypical is typical in the Sallie House. "I have seen … what I call disturbances," Leiker said. "It's similar to when you're out on the road and you see water on the road. [In the house] you can't see the wall normally. There's something there." Could it be Sallie? Maybe. According to Miller's Paranormal Research, a girl named Sallie died there. In the late 1800s, the house belonged to a doctor; late one night, a couple brought their seriously ill six-year-old daughter, Sallie, to him for help. The doctor determined that she needed emergency surgery—however, the child didn't survive the procedure. The first report of Sallie's ghost was in the early 1990s when the young daughter of a family living in the house had experiences with an entity she called Sallie—she even played with it. Sightings of Sallie continued into the late 1990s when then-resident Tony Pickman saw the girl. "Somewhere along the line the haunting picked up the name 'the Sallie house' because of the girl Tony saw," Leiker said. "A couple of psychics brought in independently gave the name of a little girl to be that of Sallie." But Leiker isn't sure the figure was actually the ghost of a little girl. "Our researchers were unable to find any information to confirm who [it is] or where she came from," she said. "Was Sallie a little girl spirit that for some reason stayed at the house, or was it the work of a demon that showed itself to be much less threat than the reality? It is possible that a demonic entity may have produced an innocent little girl named Sallie just to throw off those brought in to investigate this house and its haunting."

EVPs—electronic voice phenomenon—have been around since Thomas Edison invented sound recording. Many paranormal investigators collect EVPs by leaving audio recorders alone in a quiet room. Sometimes the recorders pick up a voice or a natural sound that should not—could not—be there. Leiker and other investigators have collected EVPs in the Sallie House. "We've gotten lots and lots of EVPs out of the place," she said. "When we first went there it was, 'I have some rocks,' like they were going to throw rocks at us. And another said, 'I have a shotgun.' But we have more luck getting EVPs if we talk about some of the more wealthy people who've lived in Atchison. One time we mentioned the Stewart House and we heard one of the little kids say, 'Can we go?'" Through EVPs, Leiker has communicated with seven entities who are regular visitors in the house: a young slave, Johanna Barnes and her son, Frank, a woman named Elizabeth, a toddler, a man named Brandon, and Sallie herself. "But we don't hear too much from Sallie," she said, although some of the entities have asked for sandwiches. Marble has also recorded EVPs. "We got a little boy's voice and a little girl's voice and I think a man's voice," she said. "Three different voices from upstairs." And, much like Leiker's experience, the voices interacted with her. "Most of the time they join our conversation," she said. "We have lots of EVPs where we're discussing something and a voice comes in commenting. It's kind of cool they kind of interact with us that way."

But Leiker discovered the spirits interact with her in a way that is not so cool. "Some of the same voices at the Sallie House I record at my own house," she said. "It must have come home with me." It always happens the same way. The telephone rings; it's Leiker's husband and he's leaving work. Leiker tells him she plans to go to the Sallie House later, then she hears the sound. "As [her husband] is talking to me I will hear an extension pick up in my house," she described. "I'll walk through [my] house looking for the extension and when I get right to that room, it hangs up. I know someone was on there." But the entity never stays in her house—it trails her as she makes the half-hour drive from Topeka to Atchison. "I've turned the corner about two blocks from the Sallie House and my cell phone could have rung," she said. "I'll hear static or silence and there's no record of that call. Even when the phone rings it doesn't ring normally." The telephone phenomena, Leiker said, has happened to other paranormal investigators who frequent the house.

But one point all the investigators agree on is that something evil lies in the basement.

While they were building the house, the Finney family lived in the basement while they worked on the rest of the home. The basement later became, as many basements do, a storage place for canning and tools, and a haven during storms. But in the late 1990s and early 2000s, the basement was used for something sinister. "After … someone else moved into the house, they were involved in some sort of ritual," Leiker said. "There was a pentagram on the basement floor. Whatever [entity] was there, was on the land originally. But it didn't have the power it had now. It got it from the ritual." A psychic in Marble's research group came to the same conclusion. "Misty [Maeder] felt someone had practiced some witchcraft or messed with the occult down there," she recounted. "She said there was something in the basement that was not very good. Sometimes it's best to ignore those types of energies because the more you focus on them, the more power you give them." And they're not alone. Leiker said every paranormal group that comes to the house has the same reaction to the basement. "There is something in the basement the psychics say is inhuman," she said. "It does seem that any psychic that comes in there … the better they are, the more they're affected. They stop short of saying it's demonic. It's inhuman."

Through the EVPs Leiker has collected, she has realized the ghostly entities in the Sallie House are aware of the inhuman thing in the basement—and they're afraid of it. "I don't know what it is, it's just really, really nasty," she said. "The entities in the house refer to it as Grandpa. The adult [spirits] tell [the child spirits] not to disturb Grandpa. There's some unknown thing in the basement that is very powerful." The thing in the basement has never confronted Leiker, so she didn't believe in its existence for a long time. But when psychic after psychic said the same thing—there's something evil down there—she started to believe. "That's just a comment that everyone makes," she said. "We have a psychic who lives in California and he can pick it up from California. That's bad."

Tony and Debra Pickman may have met that demonic force up close—it attacked Tony on several occasions. The Fox Network program *Sightings* (later on SciFi Channel) investigated the Sallie House in 1996 and captured an attack on tape. "They captured the scratches that happened on Tony," Leiker said of the claw marks that appeared to have been painfully raked across Tony's body. "We're still investigating that. I don't think the ghosts would have done it." That leaves the demonic entity in the basement. "[Tony] would be scratched right in front of us," she said. "He was not physically trying to pull any kind of trickery. The times he's been scratched, the [entity] we're most suspicious of [the thing in the basement] has said, 'I didn't do it, he did it himself.'"

The Pickmans have ceased giving interviews. "Honestly, after so many years of telling our story … it has never really been presented the way it should be, which is quite daunting to us," Debra Pickman said. "It is for this reason that my husband and I have decided not to take part in further collaborative efforts." Leiker said the move was for privacy and for their reputation. "In the beginning, the Pickmans wanted to keep their identity a secret since they live in such a small town and just didn't want criticism on top of trying to deal with living in the home," Leiker said. "Word leaked out anyway, then it seemed that trying to keep their name a secret actually made people think they were trying to hide something or that it was a sham. Many people have experienced very unexplained activity in the house reassuring the Pickmans that there was really something there."

Evah Cray Home
The Evah C. Cray Historical Home Museum sits among a flock of Victorian homes on Fifth Street. But the twenty-five-room mansion is a little different from other homes on the block. It has a three-story castle-like tower, a carriage house, and a ghost. Jane Amthor has worked at the Cray museum since 1993 and she is certain it's haunted. Things move in the Evah C. Cray Home—like an old Bible. "It was up on top of an organ and we took it and put it out on display," Amthor said. The organ is tall, but not tall enough that the Bible was hidden. "Pretty soon it was back on the organ again. We put it on display and then it was in the

The twenty-five-room Evah C. Cray Historical Home Museum sits among a flock of Victorian homes on Fifth Street in Atchison, Kansas.

back of a cabinet. Then we put it on display again and now it's gone."

The Bible isn't alone; other things in the Cray house like to roam. "We had rugs that moved around, too," Amthor explained. "She didn't want anyone to trip." The 'she' is Mrs. Evah C. Cray—who's been dead since 1993. The rug, with stitching that reads "Where Angels Tread," disappeared one day and wound up in a closet on the second floor. Ruth Stein, who has worked at the museum since 2000, said the evidence points to an otherworldly culprit. "The stuff that happens … there were only two keys, so there couldn't have been anyone doing it," Stein said. "Some of this stuff is just so weird." Amthor agreed. "You can't find a logical explanation."

The Cray house was built at the site of the earliest cemetery in Atchison, a tombstone at the side of the house reads "Atchison's first cemetery: after the city was platted, 1856." A short stone wall—like those used to outline cemeteries at the time—surrounds the property and may be another explanation for the mysterious happenings in the Cray house. "We just wonder if there aren't some bodies out there," Stein said. The Crays bought the house—built in 1882—in 1978 to use as a museum and never lived in the house. The Crays founded Atchison's Midwestern Grain Products and owned McCormick Distilling Company in nearby Weston, Missouri, until 1991. Mrs. Cray's husband, Cloud Cray, died in 1979. "Mrs. Cray gave tours up until she was eighty-eight years old," said Bobbie Wagner, who has worked in the museum since 1999. "She was a mighty little lady."

Wagner said the ghostly occurrences point to Mrs. Cray, especially because of the carriage house. "Mrs. Cray had a general store out there in '92," Wagner said. "In '99 we decided to convert it into a viewing room." The "viewing room" is a small theater in the former carriage house and later the general store. Wooden troughs and feed shoots still decorate the interior of the building. Mrs. Cray, originally from Oklahoma, loved horses and, obviously, still does. "All her horse things were on the wall and she got mad [when the building was remodeled]," Wagner said. "We'd messed up her place." Audio speakers have fallen off the wall in the viewing room, the door of a just-made custom cabinet was found hanging by one hinge, and the new projector had to be replaced—five times. But the most compelling evidence came from one of the Cray's relatives. "They were having a club meeting in the theater one evening and she [the relative] didn't believe in ghosts," Stein said. "[Club members] were exchanging decorated cookies and something trips her and all her cookies go on the floor." There was nothing on the floor to trip her. "She went and got a cup of coffee and it happened again," Stein said. "She came out and said, 'Ruth, I think you were right.'"

But since Stein, Wagner, and Amthor moved Mrs. Cray's tack and horse memorabilia into a prominent place in one of the tower rooms, the strange occurrences have stopped.

"We can only think she's happy now," Stein said. "She'll let us know if she's not."

Workers at the Evah C. Cray Historical Home Museum believe the ghost of Mrs. Evah C. Cray haunts the old mansion.

14

Ridgley Cemetery and Hell Town

Ridgley, Missouri   61.43 miles from home

At one time, Ridgley (population 64) was known by another name. "It used to be called the Hell Town because it was wild," Tammy Lanier, a ghost hunter from nearby Edgerton said. The area in northeastern Platte County, Missouri (which American Indian tribes sold for $7,500), was settled in 1841 when James F. Adams opened a saddle shop. The town of Ridgley soon grew, but after only a few years of quiet living and church picnics, Ridgley became a haven for gamblers and drunks. Saloons and gambling houses sprang up in the town, and with them came the gunfights that earned Ridgley the name Hell Town, USA. "The little town became a place of refuge for gambling and men of questionable reputation," according to a history by the Platte County Historical Society. "Men's blood was heated by the fiery whiskey that seared their throats. Tempers flared, guns spoke, and men fell dead. Fresh graves were dug in the new cemetery and loved ones mourned their dead." But the railroad, completed in 1871, bypassed Ridgley for nearby Edgerton and Hell Town dried up. "The railroad went through," Lanier said, "now it's about four houses." It wasn't until 1978 that Ridgley reinstated its city government, which had been absent since the 1920s.

Lanier, of nearby Edgerton (a comparative metropolis with a population of 533), is fascinated with one aspect of Ridgley—the cemetery's spectral resident, the White Lady.

A stone arch stands next to Route B in Platte County at the mouth of the property that has been a burial place since 1820. The cemetery's one semifamous "resident" is a niece of Davy Crockett. I met

Lanier and fellow ghost hunter Beverly Slocombe at Slocombe's house in Edgerton—they were waiting for me on the front porch smoking cigarettes. The cemetery sounded mysterious, a tribute to the colorful history of the tiny town. We pulled into the cemetery on a warm June evening, dusk flirting with the horizon. Newer graves in the still-used cemetery line the front of the property. Older graves sit at the back, where a line of trees borders the property of Slocombe's cousin Lonnie Williams. "A lot of this land was owned by a guy named [Captain Charles F.] Chrisman," said Williams, who has lived next to the cemetery all his life. "[He] donated it to people in the Civil War era who couldn't afford to be buried." The newer section was a gift from Samuel J. Peterson in memory of his "sainted mother." A wide strip of grass separates the old and new sections, and will probably always be covered with grass. "They won't allow anyone to be buried back here," Williams said. "I guess there were so many people buried with a wooden cross that rotted away, they don't know how many are out there." Records show there are 328 graves in the cemetery, but with lost graves—along with many American Indian burials—no one knows how many bodies are there. With the number of people who died during Ridgley's Hell Town days, historians speculate that there are graves on top of graves.

The Lady in White haunts Ridgley Cemetery in Ridgley, Missouri, which, in its early days was known as "Hell Town."

We drove past the newer headstones and through the just-mowed grass to the original section of the cemetery, dates as old as 1860 still visible on some weatherworn stones. Golden light from the setting sun cast long shadows across the headstones, the occasional moo from cattle in a nearby field breaking the silence. But Ridgley Cemetery isn't always so peaceful—sometimes the former residents of Hell Town, USA, are restless. Slocombe and Lanier have witnessed it firsthand.

Cemeteries don't bother Slocombe; she grew up next to Platte City Cemetery. Ghosts don't bother her either. As a child on a sleepover, she witnessed a cereal bowl levitate in her friend's kitchen. Her friend's mother said, "Put that down" and the bowl sank slowly to the counter. "It stuck with me the rest of my life," Slocombe said. But she said there's something different about the cemetery in Ridgley. "I was never afraid of graveyards until the last time we went out there," she explained. "I don't think my husband will let me take one of our vehicles out there. It broke a window." In October 2007, about ten o'clock at night, Slocombe, Lanier and a few fellow ghost hunters sat in Slocombe's car smoking. They usually stood around Slocombe's vehicle on ghost hunts, smoking cigarettes and watching the cemetery, but that night was different. "I was too scared to get out of the car," Slocombe said. "Something was telling us not to get out of the car." And she wasn't the only one to feel it. One of the ghost hunters, armed with a camera, was frozen in place. "She didn't want to roll down the windows to take pictures," Lanier said.

Then they saw the most visible denizen of the Ridgley cemetery, the White Lady—a fog-like phenomenon that moves—sometimes with intelligence. "It was like looking through Saran Wrap," Slocombe said, describing the White Lady. "It was blurry and it moved." They sat in the car, the one with the camera trying—and failing—to get a picture of the apparition through the closed window. "Then the back window of my vehicle went *reeennnttt*," Slocombe said, describing the sound of a car window being forced down. But the car's engine was off, so the electric window couldn't have worked. One of the other ghost hunters "almost leaped into the front with us," Lanier said. Slocombe started the car and shoved it into drive—but it wouldn't move. She could hear the engine running, but as she hammered the gas peddle, the engine noise didn't fluctuate. "I could hear it running and it just didn't move. It didn't even rev," she said. "I took my foot off the gas, hit it again and it took off." Undeterred, Slocombe and Lanier have been back to the Ridgley cemetery, and have seen the White Lady on a few other rare occasions.

One night at about eleven o'clock, Slocombe and other ghost hunters were standing around their vehicle smoking cigarettes when Slocombe saw the White Lady. "I kept seeing something out by the tree line," she said. "It was a white figure. Human shaped." Slocombe tried to focus on the figure, but it was difficult. "It would disappear and show up again," she said. "I only saw it three times. Each time it came back it was closer. At that point I told them, 'Let's go. I want to get out of here.'" And the ghost hunters tumbled into the vehicle. "When I go to shut my door a bright white light shoots past," Slocombe recalled. "I saw it, but didn't say anything. Tammy leans up and said, 'Did you see that?' She'd seen the same thing." For many nights afterward, Slocombe saw the White Lady of the Ridgley cemetery again—in her dreams. "After that I'd have dreams about her," she said. "And in my dreams I saw it in slow motion. It was a white lady and she was screaming as she went by."

We didn't see the White Lady that night. Lights from airliners preparing to land at nearby Kansas City International Airport were the only lights streaking above the cemetery. But sometimes you don't have to be inside the cemetery gates to see her. "I've seen it once standing on the side of the road in the grass," Lanier said. "But I've only seen it like that once." If you are ever by Ridgley, slow down and look as you pass the lonely little cemetery—something might be looking at you, too.

15

O'Malley's 1842 Irish Pub

Tree-filled hills embrace the entrance to Weston in northwest Missouri and guide drivers quietly into town, past a speckling of homes and a road sign reading "Weston: Population 1,631." Other signs soon sprout among the trees: McCormick Distillery, Pirtle Winery, Weston Brewing Company. In the 1800s, Weston—known as the Queen of the Platte Purchase—sat on the banks of the Missouri River, welcoming hundreds of steamboats filled with entrepreneurs and adventurers traveling west. In its heyday, the town's population swelled to more than 5,000. Some famous residents of early Weston were descendents of Daniel Boone; Elijah Cody, uncle of Buffalo Bill Cody; Ben Holladay, founder of the McCormick Distillery; and Mary (Owens) Vineyard, who turned down future president Abraham Lincoln's marriage proposal because she thought him a bore. Some of those long-dead residents may still be there.

This frontier town, established in 1837, has also seen tragedy. Civil War border skirmishes between Missouri and Kansas pitted families and neighbors against each other. A business district fire in 1855 almost erased the town. The Missouri River—the lifeblood of Weston— decimated the town with floods in 1858 and 1881; the latter flood changed the course of the river away from town, which crippled its economy. Some of the pain from death and disaster may still be lurking in Weston. And as with many other spirits, it's waiting at the pub.

German immigrant John Georgian established the Weston Brewing Company in 1842. Georgian had workers dig stone cellars to keep the colder-fermenting German lager beer at a constant temperature; these cellars are still used as tavern rooms for what is now O'Malley's 1842 Irish Pub at 500 Welt Street. Fire destroyed the first brewery build-

Irish balladeer Bob Reeder plays O'Malley's 1842 Irish Pub in Weston, Missouri, as he has every Sunday since 1987.

ing in 1860. In the early 1900s, the brewery produced a Western Royal beer that was known internationally, and during Prohibition, it produced a non-alcoholic beer. Today, the Weston Brewing Company operates O'Malley's, which features microbrews O'Malley's SunRye's Ale, O'Malley's Cream Ale, O'Malley's Emerald Lager, and O'Malley's Irish Style Bitter.

A flight of stairs descends from the entrance of O'Malley's to an arched brick-lined tunnel leading to the pub's uppermost cellar, and to more stairs leading down to the lower cellar. Cold water drips on patrons' heads as they pass through the dark, lonely tunnel before entering a warm room filled with music and laughter. Irish flags and advertisements for Harp Lager Beer and Guinness dot the brick and mortar walls meeting overhead in a low arch. The room boasts its historical roots with a sign declaring "cockfighting," a map of the Louisiana Purchase (of which Missouri was a part), and a Rebel flag.

Cigarette smoke layers the air of this Irish bar like the black and tans featured on its menu. The menu also features beer ranging from Guinness Extra Stout to Miller Lite, and drinks like The O'Malley, made of Guinness, vodka, and Tabasco. The smallest entry on the menu is food. O'Malley's offers the Pub Sandwich. Period. Ham, turkey, or corned beef dressed with Swiss cheese and mustard served warm with potato chips and a pickle.

Dark wooden tables marred with dents and the rings of thousands of drinks sit between high-backed benches so tall the crests of patrons' heads barely show over the top. Cigarette smoke shoots from behind those bench backs like blasts from a gun. A waitress calling patrons "Hon" sets oaken bowls of pretzels on the tables, the hollow *thunk* of wood-upon-wood barely audible over the music and the laughter.

Irish balladeer Bob Reeder plays in this room on Sunday afternoons. Thirty-some people sit and chat, some complacently listening to Reeder, some singing along, and all drinking Bud Light, dark black Guinness, or various shades of the house beers. But all come to attention as the red-bearded, bespectacled man in a vest and British driving cap finishes a song and speaks. "This [next song] requires audience participation in two parts," Reeder says, holding up two fingers. "'Irish dynamiters' and 'Not much cake.'" People laugh and clap as Reeder starts to play, waiting for their cue to yell, "Irish dynamiters." When it comes and a mumble fumbles its way into the air, Reeder stops playing. "That sucked," he says, a great smile growing behind his beard. He starts again while the audience hoots and laughs.

Reeder has performed Irish folk tunes at O'Malley's for twenty-two years. He has met an uncountable number of people there, but one encounter at the pub has remained with him for decades— meeting the pub ghost. "When I first started here I worked the grand opening," he said. "The tunnel wasn't opened yet. The floor bricks weren't here; there was just gravel on the floor." The tunnel entrance was blocked to keep people from entering because there was no way out. "I was playing and turned and looked down the tunnel. It was closed off with two boards, like this," he said, crossing his arms into an X. "I could see somebody looking back at me."

The spot where Reeder performs is near the tunnel entrance, separated by a table and space to walk around it, so the view was clear. "Somebody was looking back at me," Reeder said. "It kind of spooked me and I took a break shortly thereafter because there wasn't any way to get down there. You couldn't get there from here or from the other end." But someone, or something, was there—he is certain of that. "It was a face of someone that was looking at me. Just the face. Kind of a white face. The eyes were …" he recalled, pausing to stroke the hair on his chin. "How do I describe this? They were *intensely* looking at me. I don't know what sex the ghost, or entity, or whatever I saw, was. It was just a face." Reeder's hand slowly dropped to the table and the smile again took control of his face. "I wasn't drinking that night." Reeder told the owner about the encounter and "he kind of laughed at me and didn't think much of it."

But Reeder knew what he saw because he had experienced the unexplainable before. "I've seen several things in my life," he said. "It started when I was a kid. I had an accident." The young Reeder hit himself in the back of the head with the blade of a hatchet. "I didn't know what happened," he said. "I put my hand on the back of the head and it was covered with blood." Reeder pointed to a spot below his right ear. "It split my skull right there." His parents took him inside the house and as they were debating what to do, Reeder left his body. "I was flying above my bed as they were deciding whether to take me to the hospital or not," he explained. "I was floating. I could see myself in bed."

Reeder's parents took him to the hospital, but later, after he healed, he realized something was different—he started having new experiences. "I had another experience as a kid," he said. "I was called up in the attic. I was just called." Reeder left his bed in the darkness and walked up to the attic where he saw something that shouldn't have been there. "There were three what I might call ghosts," he said. "They had triangular heads and shadowed bod[ies]." Reeder and these entities stared at one another until his father walked in. "My father came up," he said. "He found I was out of bed and looked for me. When he came up the stairs he saw me looking at something in the corner." But when Reeder's father got close, "the entities turned into each other and disappeared."

The sighting at O'Malley's was not the lone supernatural encounter Reeder had at the pub. Three years after he saw the face in the tunnel, four women from the Navajo Nation visited O'Malley's, sat at the table next to the tunnel, and told Reeder something that chilled

It was in this underground brick tunnel, which leads to one of the bar's rooms, that Bob Reeder saw the pub ghost in 1987.

him. "They were shaman women," he said. "One of them looked at me and said, 'This place is haunted.' I said, 'No it's not.' She said, 'Yes, it is. It's standing over there in this tunnel.'" Reeder looked down the tunnel and saw the same entity he had seen years before staring back at him.

Since then he has researched the brewing company history and found evidence it could be haunted. "In 1893, there was a fire," he said. "Several people lost their lives right there in the tunnel. In 1889 there was an earthquake. In 1916, a murder." Employees have also reported hearing wooden barrels rolling in the cellars "like in the old days," witnessing objects as large as a loaf of bread move by itself, and a few have reported seeing a strange woman in the pub after hours. But despite the reports of noises, levitating objects, and the face staring at Reeder from the darkness, he is at peace with whatever haunts O'Malley's 1842 Irish Pub. "No ominous feeling. Whatever it was, was glad we were all here," Reeder said. "It wasn't meant to scare me. It was meant to let me know something was there. When I walked in this place the first time, it was like there was somebody welcoming me. That's why I've stayed. I wouldn't mind dying here. If I was going to die, this is the place I'd do it."

People cheered and beer glasses clanked as Reeder started back to his place under the lights, but he stopped and turned around. "I'd better get one more," he said, walking back to the bar and coming back with a pint of beer. He pulled his guitar over his shoulder, smiled at the crowd, and sang "Danny Boy." All conversation stopped; the bar crowd just sat and listened. When he was finished, the room erupted in applause. A man walked up to Reeder and slipped some money into the tip jar. "Thank you very much," Reeder said, the smile that rarely leaves his face welcoming the man. "The dogs will eat now."

16

An Encounter
with a Black-Eyed Kid

There is something wrong with these children. They approach quietly, but boldly. They are usually teens or slightly younger. They insist on coming inside your house to use the bathroom, the telephone, or just for a drink of water. But for some reason you are afraid. Why? They're just kids. Then you notice their eyes—black, as if the pupil had poured over its banks. You don't let them in—do you?

Black-Eyed Kids. The term has floated across cyberspace since January 16, 1998, when journalist Brian Bethel first posted his chilling encounter with overly lucid children whose eyes were completely black; not a hint of iris or white. And they scared the hell out of him. The existence of these children has since become an Internet urban legend, but is it really just that? Maybe not. Hundreds of people have posted their encounters with Black-Eyed Kids online—all of them claiming a feeling of dread caused them to close the door in these children's faces.

But what are these Black-Eyed Kids? Speculation ranges from demons to drugs. All-black contact lenses are readily available, and certain narcotics can cause the pupil to dilate to dimensions uncomfortable to look at. As online poster Shaun Wingle relates, "Pupils can be extremely big when one ingests psychedelic mushrooms. I remember the one time I was on them, I looked at myself in the mirror, and I could see no color of eyes save a very small sliver of an outline of my blue iris." Wingle had ingested the mushrooms during the daylight hours. "If in complete darkness, I'm sure the pupil might have been a tad bit bigger. Meth makes your pupils pretty big, but not as big as mushrooms. There's a lot of nifty trippers out there that wouldn't hurt a fly."

However, it's the paranormal aspect that sends chills through those exploring Black-Eyed Kids. Online poster JillyAn and her cousin have developed a hypothesis about these entities. "You know how you hear stories about people just dropping dead in their homes or running off the road in their cars and being killed?" she asked. "Everybody always says, 'Gee, we don't know what happened. He/she was fine yesterday.' My cousin said, 'What if they were approached by one of these things and they let it in? Maybe these thing are death.' That makes some sense to me."

Guy Malone of the Alien Resistance in Roswell, New Mexico, said these Black-Eyed entities could be satanic in origin. "Going by the fruits described—terror—I would imagine any such manifestations are probably demonic or fallen angel-related," Malone theorized. "If I encountered such an entity and it seemed fearful or threatening, I would probably attempt to rebuke it in the authority of Jesus Christ and judge the results accordingly."

What follows is a story of a Black-Eyed Kid who showed up at the door of a house in a small Missouri town. "Beth" and "Ellen" are pseudonyms: Beth requested anonymity because she is worried about the safety of her children. She doesn't fully understand what happened, but she knows that drugs and black contact lenses cannot explain the little girl who came to her door and brought terror into her life.

The knock on the front door was strange in itself. One day in early April 2009, Beth, a stay-at-home mom, was in the kitchen making lunch when she heard a knock on the front door. No one comes to the front door. "We usually use the back door and everyone we know knows that, and we hardly ever get visitors at the front," she said. "I opened the door and there was a little girl standing there. I did not recognize her." Lawson is a small town of about 2,300 people where everyone knows everyone. "She was about seven years old and she was staring down at her shoes," Beth said. "She had blond hair and was dressed in an antique-type dingy white dress with blue embroidery birds at the edges."

Beth opened the screen door and knelt to talk to the girl. She was worried the girl was hurt or in danger. "She looked at my hands and said, 'I need help. Can I come inside, please?'" Beth said. "She was so polite and spoke so well. She did not sound as if she was from around town. I suddenly felt very afraid." Beth looked up and down the street, but no one was around. "I looked past her, thinking the fear I felt must be someone after her or that her parents or someone must be upset with me talking to her," she said. "Thoughts raced through my mind quickly and I somehow could not think very clearly all of a sudden."

Beth looked back at the girl preparing to ask where her parents were and where she lived when she noticed the little girl's eyes. "She looked at me and I immediately noticed that her eyes seemed wrong or something," she said. "Like they were ink. Like someone had poured ink in her eyes. They were not normal kids eyes. They were coal black, and black from rim-to-rim, just staring." The girl again demanded to come inside. "I could hear a kind of fake sweetness in her voice. She had a little girl voice but had an adult vocabulary and force about her," Beth said. "I immediately stood up and knew I needed to protect myself and my girls inside and started to close the door."

The girl asked what she had done wrong; why Beth wouldn't invite her in. "That is when my five-year-old daughter came into the living room and I knew that she should not look at her," Beth said. "I closed the door on this little girl and I locked it. I scooped up Ellen and ran to the back door in the kitchen. I locked it and sat down at the table. My sixteen-month-old was sleeping upstairs and I needed to check her." Beth ran upstairs on shaking legs, holding Ellen tightly in her arms. The baby was still asleep. "I got my cell phone out and called my husband and told him about it," she said. "He thinks my story is crazy."

But Beth knows the little Black-Eyed girl was on her porch, and she knows the terror she felt. "This little girl was real. I had started to feel sorry for her because she had bad breath and really dirty hair," Beth said. "But I somehow know that she meant harm to us. I am not sure if I want to talk too much about it anymore. I would rather forget that it happened at all, but I worry that she will return." Hours after the encounter with the Black-Eyed Kid, the fear remained. "I won't let the girls play outside now," she said. "I have not gone out by myself to the store or anything. I still feel that dread, that sense of fear I felt emanating from the girl on my porch. I somehow knew that if I had let her in, that I would have regretted it and my girls and I would have been in some sort of real danger."

17

The Jesse James Farm and Museum

Frank and Jesse James were bad men—thieves, killers, and outlaws. But despite Frank and Jesse James's bloodthirsty nature, many Americans considered the brothers to be heroes. Historian Thomas Holloway said the popular press at the time, and much later Hollywood, painted these bank and train robbers with a romantic hue, which was far from the truth. "Jesse James was a cold-blooded murderer," he said. "He was not a Robin Hood." Jesse James has been dead since 1882, Frank since 1915, but despite this, many people have reported seeing, hearing, and feeling the James brothers to this day. Do the James brothers haunt those places familiar to them in life? Maybe they're planning their next robbery, or maybe they're simply afraid of the rest of their journey. But the James family, and someone closely tied to them, clearly aren't ready to move on to the other side.

A dirt trail brushes a creek as it winds from the Jesse James Farm and Museum, under trees and finally to the house where Jesse Woodson James and his brother Frank, two of the most notorious and deadly outlaws in American history, played as boys. A break in the fence that surrounds the farmhouse allows visitors to climb the thick wooden steps to the lawn of the Jesse James home. Save for the occasional tour group, the scant white house where Jesse was born (Frank was born in Kentucky) sits in silence. Robberies were planned in that house, and an attack there by the Pinkerton Detective Agency injured the boys' mother, Zerelda, and killed their half-brother, Archie Samuel. Frank died at the house and Jesse was buried in the yard before his remains were moved to Mount Olivet Cemetery in

The graves of Jesse and Zerelda James at Mt. Olivet Cemetery in Kearney, Missouri. Jesse, Frank, and others associated with the James brothers are said to haunt the old James home.

Kearney. Since Clay County purchased the home to turn it into a historic site in 1978, some tour guides have claimed that although the James boys have long since died, they have never left. When historical interpreter Stephanie Gaddis started work at the James Farm, she didn't believe in the ghosts of the James boys—but she quickly found out that they believe in her.

Ghost hunters, psychics, and tour guides have reported experiencing something otherworldly in the home. However, Gaddis (from nearby Holt, Missouri) never considered ghosts to be real—until she worked at the farm. "I was working one day and I walked through the house," she said. "We always go through the house [from the rear entrance] and walk through the parlor and go through Frank's room to let people in." The interior of the James home is dark in the mornings. A bed where Frank slept still sits in the front room, along with pieces of period furniture, a number of them donated by the James's descendents. It was here Gaddis experienced something she didn't expect. "I heard footsteps like people were walking in behind me," Gaddis said. "I thought people were pulling a prank. I looked back in the room to see if someone was there, but it was empty. It sounded like somebody walking across the floor. It was heavy steps, not light." As she stood in Frank's room, inches from the bed where a killer once slept, the thump of boots grew closer. "I've never seen a ghost in my life and I don't believe in ghosts," she said. "I thought it's probably my tour group on the front porch." She pushed back the curtains, but the group was still coming up the dirt path. Gaddis opened the front door and let her group in. They filed up the steps, and walked over the wood-planked porch and into Frank's room. "Then I heard it again," she said, the loud, heavy steps of a boot-clad man. "I asked if the [group] heard it and they said 'yes.' They said they thought it was somebody in the house ready to jump out and scare us like they were Jesse." They went through the house and found no one who was trying to frighten them. So whom did those boots belong to? Jesse? Frank? Or someone who long ago walked onto the property looking for the James boys—and never walked off?

Some people at the farm—tour guides and visitors alike—have heard voices, and some have seen furniture move by itself. Historian Thomas Holloway has seen an apparition. From 2002 to 2005, Holloway worked as a historical interpreter at the farm, and studied the James family, but mostly Frank James, and Frank's wife, Annie. Annie may have liked the attention because in 2004, Holloway met her. One early spring morning, Holloway was sitting on the front steps of the home waiting for guests to arrive when he saw someone coming up the walk … alone. She approached Holloway and stopped about twenty feet from him. "Standing out in front of me was the figure of a woman," he said. "A rather small woman wearing a straight black dress of the period. It occurred to me at the time, 'My God, that's Annie,' then …" Holloway snapped his fingers, "she was gone. But it was so clear." Although Frank enjoyed the attention the farm drew after Jesse's death, Annie didn't. Frank would greet visitors by the front gate and give tours of the farm. Annie hated being a celebrity, so she stayed at the farmhouse. "I recognized the person," Holloway said. "I knew who it had to be."

Although Gaddis is still not sure about the existence of ghosts, she knows there is something strange about that house. "The house just kind of makes you feel nervous when you're in there by yourself," she said. "It makes you [feel] kind of eerie."

18

Oujia Boards

The Ouija board—a playing surface now usually made from cardboard and decorated with the alphabet, the numbers one through ten, and the words "yes" and "no"—has existed in its current design since 1890, although similar incarnations of these "witch boards" have been around for at least 2,500 years. The board, used to make contact with the spirit world, was made popular during the Spiritualist movement of the late 1800s, after novelty toy company owner Charles Kennard patented the design and called the board "Ouija." But although it was—and still is—sold as a toy, the Ouija board is viewed as a tool to make contact with the dead or, as many claim, demonic forces. One of the more famous cases of Ouija board contact occurred in the early 1900s when Mark Twain supposedly spoke to a woman from his hometown of Hannibal, Missouri.

Between 1915 and 1917, Emily Grant Hutchings, a struggling novelist, teacher, and writer for St. Louis newspapers, claimed Mark Twain dictated his last novel and two short stories—"Daughter of Mars" and "Up the Furrow to Fortune"—to her one letter at a time through a Ouija board. "They got on the Ouija board and supposedly had this conversation," said Henry Sweets, curator of the Twain Museum in Hannibal. Many conversations. Twain supposedly dictated chapter after chapter—including revisions—to Hutchings and spiritualist medium Lola V. Hays, according to Hutchings' forward in the book.

The book, *The Coming of Jap Herron*, was published by Mitchell Kennerley in 1917 as "a novel written from the Ouija board—Mark Twain via Emily Grant Hutchings." Harper & Brothers, owners of the copyright on the pen name "Mark Twain," sued Kennerley in 1918. Given the nature of Ouija boards—although not officially classified as a game by the Supreme Court until 1920—Harper & Brothers had a strong case. But according to a story in the July 28, 1918, *New York*

Times, the case was about more than an issue of copyright. "We will put the issue up to the Supreme Court," said James N. Rosenberg, an attorney for Harper & Brothers. "We will have a final ruling on immortality."

Part of Harper & Brothers' case revolved around the fact that Twain had written in the books *What is Man?* and *The Mysterious Stranger* that he didn't acknowledge life after death. According to the publisher's attorney, "He [Twain] refused to believe in a spirit world," the *New York Times* reported. "He refused to be a spook. Judge or jury must weigh that fact." But the case never went to trial, and life after death remains in the realm of religion. Kennerley and Hutchings agreed to stop distribution of *Jap Herron* and to destroy all known copies, and Harper & Brothers dropped the lawsuit.

So the question remains: was the novel written by Mark Twain? In *Contact with the Other World* (1919), prominent psychic researcher and well-known esoteric writer James H. Hyslop details many sessions with Hays and Hutchings at a Ouija board and describes evidence that Mark Twain had dictated a book from the Great Beyond. And he may have dictated a book ... maybe even two.

Independence, Missouri   80 miles from home

God Bless U, Daughter
Mark Twain died in 1910. During the mid- to late-1800s, Twain's novels, essays, and short stories made him a worldwide celebrity. Through financial failures and personal tragedy, Twain—who in 1875 pecked out the first novel ever written on a typewriter, *The Adventures of Tom Sawyer*—never stopped writing. Maybe even after death.

In the late 1960s, Independence, the quiet home of former president Harry S. Truman, who still took strolls around the town square, was visited by another famous Missourian. Marcene Boothe remembers those visits—they were in her neighborhood. "We had a next-door neighbor that talked to Mark Twain with a 'Nona Board,'" she said. The "Nona Board" was a type of Ouija board created by her neighbors, John and Mildred Swanson. Mildred Swanson once wrote that she and John created the board because the word Ouija means

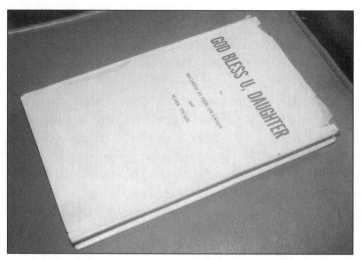

John and Mildred Swanson's Midwest Society of Psychic Research claimed to regularly talk with Mark Twain during séances in the late 1960s. Mildred wrote *God Bless U, Daughter* about her conversations with the author.

"yes-yes" (*Oui*: French, *Ja*: German) and "there is also need for a 'no-no' reaction." The word "Nona," she explained, came from an Egyptian seeress from "an earlier time." And with it, they and other members of Swanson's Midwest Society of Psychic Research conducted séances. "They regularly talked to Mark Twain and other deceased people," Boothe said. "She eventually wrote a book regarding these conversations [with Twain] and entitled it *God Bless U, Daughter*, as that is how Twain ended each conversation with her."

But Boothe was never invited for one of these séances. "No. Oh, no," she said. "I was never asked to join in. I think that they knew we probably wouldn't have gone along with it. She would talk about it." Mildred liked to talk. A full lot stretched between the Swanson and Boothe homes, and that's where Mildred kept her garden—an area sectioned off by a fence the Boothe children were afraid to cross to retrieve baseballs. "I wouldn't call them normal neighbors," Boothe said. "They didn't socialize with people around the neighborhood. The only time we talked was because she'd be out working in the garden."

But the Boothes became close enough to the Swansons that they received a copy of *God Bless U, Daughter*. Because the name Mark Twain was on the cover, the Swansons found the book hard to publish. "It was by Mildred Burris Swanson and Mark Twain," Boothe said. "She could not get a publisher to publish a book that was written by a deceased person as she claimed the authors to be her and Mark Twain, so she published it herself." Only the Swansons, who are now deceased, knew how many copies were sold. However, Mildred Swanson left behind a reason for seeking out Twain and writing the book. "I spent years asking a question that no living person could answer. 'Where do we go when we die?' It was important that I know because a controversy, created for me at an early age, has never been resolved," she wrote. "Mark Twain, from his home on the astral plane, with love and patience, finally restored my ordered world so that I came full circle to the origin of my problems."

Unlike *The Coming of Jap Herron*, *God Bless U, Daughter* is not a novel—it is a diary of the conversations the Swansons claim they had with Twain. Mildred Swanson claimed Twain told her of incidents before they happened, such as her mother being injured in a fall, and told her that other famous authors were watching her, such as Robert Louis Stevenson and Edgar Rice Burroughs.

A medium from Independence, Margie Kay, said both cases are legitimate. "Emily and Lola are telling the truth," she said of the *Jap Herron* readings. "They did communicate via the Ouija board. I think this one is real ... and I'd take the writings seriously." The Swanson case, Kay said, is a bit more complicated. "I see them talking about the previous case—they read about it, and may even have the book in hand," Kay said. "They were talking about how they could attract more people to join their group and thought about trying to contact Twain themselves using the same method. At first, they are not in contact with him—it may have been another spirit or no spirit at all, but later on he does come in and he is angry and amused at their shenanigans."

Despite the 1920 Supreme Court ruling on Ouija boards, in some circles these boards are not considered toys. So take care, you may conjure something a little more dangerous than a humorist from Hannibal.

Something Took My Wife

The group of friends huddled around a game board, their fingers hovering over a small flittering planchette. It was the 1960s. Roland Sneed and his then-wife were in Kansas City from Oklahoma visiting her parents when someone decided it would be fun to play with the unknown. "My former wife and I spent several hours with friends using the Ouija board," Sneed, now of Blue Springs, Missouri, said. "Sometimes the planchette went very slow, and sometimes it would go so fast that it would fly off the board. Some answers were cryptic, some muddled, and some very, very interesting."

Later, the couple slept in a seldom-used room in the old house. But the board wasn't finished playing. "My wife began making strange movements and then started talking in a voice not her own," Sneed said. "I wasn't scared, but fascinated. I started asking questions about who she was and she replied that she was an ancestor of my wife. It is hard to know whether or not this was true. Specific facts were not given." Soon after, his wife came out of the trance, "with beaded sweat on her brow and scared out of her mind," Sneed said. "She said that she could feel the spirit trying to take over her body and had struggled against it until she got back into control. She refused to even look at a Ouija board after that."

Sneed and his wife had met what Dawn Newlan, a medium with the Ozark Paranormal Society, calls lower-level energies. "Generally, the things that come through always tell you they are a friend, a family member, a whatever," Dawn said, adding that you should keep your distance. "Ouijas to me, and to most anyone who's been around one, will tell you they are very dangerous," she stated. "When someone plays with a board, they begin to open up the doorways of communication with the other side." Negative energies come through these doorways, Dawn explained. Sometimes these energies are people who were bad in life and sometimes they are demons. "Satan has his legions," Dawn said. "If you do not know how to discern good entities from bad entities, that's when you wind up with your problems. What most people don't understand is that if you ask them a question, 'Hey what is my dog's name?' [The name] is in your head. That spirit can take it out of your head and give you what you want to hear, but once it scares the hell out of you, you'll quit."

19

Fairview Cemetery and the Black Angel

The solid bronze statue of an angel, darkened by age and the elements, stands in a small, well-kept park at the edge of Fairview Cemetery. Large, graceful wings tinged in green grow from the back of the robe-clad statue. In one arm she holds a bowl, her other arm reaches out in welcome. The statue—the Ruth Anne Dodge Memorial—was dedicated in 1920 to the memory of Ruth Anne Dodge, the wife of General Grenville Dodge. Abraham Lincoln hired General Dodge as chief engineer of the Transcontinental Railroad. The angel's sculptor, Daniel Chester French, is best known for carving the statue of Abraham Lincoln that sits in the Lincoln Memorial. No one is buried at the statue (Ruth Anne Dodge isn't even buried in Fairview Cemetery—she is in the family mausoleum at Walnut Hill Cemetery a few miles away), and the statue isn't actually in the cemetery, yet the angel remains a focal point of ghostly folklore. Maybe it has to do with Mrs. Dodge's dreams.

Courtney Brummer, assistant managing editor of Council Bluffs' newspaper, *The Daily Nonpareil*, has studied the history and the haunted reputation of the Black Angel statue. "The legend has it that Ruth Anne Dodge had dreamed about this Black Angel in a boat," Brummer said, "and the Black Angel held a bowl of water." In the dream, Dodge is standing on a shore when a boat approaches through the mist. A beautiful woman stands on the boat holding a bowl in one arm while her other arm reaches out in welcome. The woman Dodge thought to be an angel asked her to drink from the bowl; Dodge didn't. The dream replayed itself the next night and

Dodge again refused to drink from the bowl. "She told her daughters if she dreamed about the angel again, she'd drink from it," Brummer said. "She died in her sleep that night." Many people speculated Dodge again dreamt of the angel that night, and this time drank from the bowl. "Legend has it if you drink from the bowl [on the statue]," Brummer said, "you'll die."

Legend has it the Black Angel statue at the Ruth Anne Dodge Memorial in Council Bluffs, Iowa, comes to life at night.

But that's only one legend. Some locals claim the statue lifts off its pedestal and flies at night, others claim it cries tears of blood, but a good number of the statue legends involve death. *Gateway*, the student newspaper at the nearby University of Nebraska–Omaha, compiled these warnings: "Any girl who is kissed at the angel's feet in the moonlight will die within six months; touching the angel on Halloween night would lead to death in seven years; kissing the angel itself would make your heart stop beating." Mollie Hotchkiss, a student at Northwest Missouri State University, grew up in the area and has heard stories like this from her family. "My mom said that my uncle and his friends in high school went to the statue late at night," she said. "They were probably drunk, we don't know; and someone looked the angel straight in the eyes and [the angel] took her head off and rolled it after them down the street."

Over the years, the angel has become a popular spot for teenagers to prove their bravery, which doesn't sit well with the locals, although many are wary of the angel themselves. "The people that live around it, they're kind of half-and-half," Brummer said. "Some say nothing happens, but others say it feels like there's a presence there. A lot of people are hesitant to talk about it because of the vandalism." In 2008, vandals painted the statue with "666," swastikas, and "die, die, die" in red spray paint; others have painted the statue white. "The urban legends lead to what people do when they deface it," Brummer said. "But that doesn't mean nothing happens." Brummer has spoken with enough people who have experienced something strange at the statue to know there's something paranormal about it. "People have reported seeing blue and white lights dancing around," she said. "The more legitimate reports are just feeling a presence and seeing the lights. Not so much orbs, but dancing lights."

But the angel is more of a prelude to the real darkness lurking next door.

~•~

A large black dog jogged shakily down a rutted gravel road, spider-webbing its way through Fairview Cemetery. Saliva foaming around its mouth, it paused to stare down my car creeping past. Jet-black squirrels, common to the area, skittered through the cemetery like shadows. Fairview Cemetery sits at the top of Oakland Avenue in Council Bluffs, its ancient headstones pouring down the hill. Once known as the Old Burying Grounds for the number of American Indians buried there, it later became a Mormon cemetery, then a city cemetery. Many of the town's early elite found their final home at Fairview, as did Civil War soldiers. At the north part of the cemetery is the Kinsman Monument, its cannon standing silent watch over their graves. "Most of the reported phenomena comes from the cemetery," Brummer said. "I've actually been out there twice for paranormal investigations."

Local paranormal investigators have detected high, unexplained electromagnetic fields near the statue and inside the cemetery; they have captured strange lights in photographs and have heard screams. SPIRAL Paranormal of Bellevue, Nebraska, investigated the statue and the cemetery in 2007 and found evidence of a haunting. "As we entered the cemetery we all felt a heaviness," paranormal investigator Shane Huggins wrote in his case report on the investigation. As they walked deeper into the graveyard, Shane and fellow investigator J. D. Hudgins saw a dark, shadowy figure moving among the headstones. "We walked briskly toward the figure—as we did this, the figure walked through a mausoleum and disappeared. We continued into the cemetery where again we noticed a shadow person or persons moving." Photographs revealed only orbs, but Shane is convinced he experienced something supernatural in the cemetery. "I felt a cold hand touch my neck," he wrote. "After about twenty steps, again I felt the hand on my neck. I then announced, 'This is my space, please do not invade my space,' and the heaviness we felt lifted. I don't feel that the haunting is that of an evil spirit as the story goes, but more of a playful human spirit trying to make contact."

Other investigators have gathered EVPs (electronic voice phenomenon), which are unexpected sounds that appear on an audio recording. Ghost hunters place tape and digital audio recorders in empty rooms and quiet cemeteries to capture the voices of earthbound spirits—and some of them are successful. Brummer said

Paranormal investigators have reported shadowy figures and disembodied voices in the Fairview Cemetery, located next to the Ruth Anne Dodge Memorial.

local paranormal research groups have captured voices of the dead in Fairview Cemetery. "They were in an area where there's a marker for an infant," she said. "It just has a first name on it. It's a foreign name. They have EVPs of the child laughing and talking to them."

Brummer has experienced strange events in the cemetery at night, such as inexplicable lights and a heavy feeling of dread that suddenly crept over her. "There's a part of the cemetery, the northeastern part of it, it's one of the older parts of the cemetery," she said. "I was talking to someone else, and it just seemed all of a sudden I have got to move from where I was standing. There's something not good here. It felt like something didn't want me where I was." Thinking she was standing on a grave, Brummer looked around, but there was no marker. Of course, a lack of marker doesn't mean she wasn't standing on a grave. "I moved probably fifteen feet and the feeling completely vanished."

Paranormal investigator Dave Christiansen from nearby Nickerson, Nebraska, said the feeling of not being wanted—a kind of heaviness or oppression in the air—is common, and people should pay attention to it because some spirit is probably trying to communicate. "The reason you're getting those creeping feelings is you're feeling someone who doesn't want you there," he said. "Whenever you go into some place and you get some feeling of dread, get out of there—even though we don't. You wouldn't believe how many ghosts are out there and some of them are very, very angry. Some are bad." And they will react if you challenge them. "We heard a couple teenagers who were up in the cemetery one night and they'd been doing a bit of drinking and a bit of smoking and they were making fun of the idea of ghosts," he reported. "One of the teenagers was physically attacked. [He] ended up with a black eye and a fat lip and bruises on [his] body. If you make fun of [the dead] and if they have the ability to strike, they will." To protect yourself, Christiansen suggests building a rapport with the spirits. "Go there during the day, talk to them and if you see any trash there, pick it up," he said. "If you see any stones knocked over, pick them up, show them you care. They start becoming more friendly to you."

Christiansen and his wife, Leslie, have "been all over God's creation" seeking out the paranormal and have investigated the Black Angel statue and Fairview Cemetery. "[The Black Angel] is nothing but folklore. There's nothing to it," he said. "But the cemetery behind it is bursting with all kinds of paranormal stuff. It's really a fascinating cemetery." Like other paranormal investigators who have investigated Fairview Cemetery, the Christiansens have captured EVPs there. "One was of a woman crying. We heard crying one time on an EVP," he said. "We've heard children laugh. One time we heard a man say, 'Should I?' And a woman said, 'No, don't.' I have a funny feeling he was trying to interact with us and the woman said leave them be." But they have also heard the voices of the dead calling at them through the night—not through an audio recorder, but through the air. "We've had people talk to us. You can hear that with your ears—that was no EVP," he reported. "We get the usual, 'Why are you here?' 'What are you looking for?' 'What is that [in regards to their equipment]?' Short little blurts referring to us. That just goes to show ghosts do interact."

But unlike the many paranormal investigators who may only pick up pictures of orbs and the occasional garbled EVP, spirits have also interacted physically with the Christiansens. "We've had equipment get destroyed," he said. "EMF [electromagnetic field] meters and video cameras just burned out. We don't know how, why, or what." One night the Christiansens were using a 35 mm camera and when they took the film to be developed the next day, the negatives came out blank. "We asked the guy what could have caused this," Christiansen said. "He said if it was still in your camera, it was hit with a high level of radiation." Christiansen said he and his wife experienced a warm sensation at one point during that investigation that was immediately followed by an intense cold. He wonders what may have passed through them that night.

One of the dangers of investigating the unknown, Christiansen said, is bringing your work home with you. "The bad thing about doing what we do is a lot of times you bring people home with you," he said. "Sometimes things will get attached to you because you remind them of somebody or you showed some interest in them. The count of spirits in our house is ten." One of the spirits is a little girl named Crystal. "We bought her a Christmas present one year and we got an EVP of her singing 'Here Comes Santa Claus,'" Christiansen said. Leslie and Dave call Crystal and the other spirits that haunt their home roommates, and they expect to have more. "If you have a ghost in your house, you'll have more over time," he said. "They'll travel down the street and if they see one in a house, they'll go in there just to talk. They'll stay together whether they like each other or not. It's for companionship."

Although spirits of the dead don't seem to be bound to any one area, if they could go anywhere, why are they hanging out at Fairview or any other cemetery? "Not all of them do," Christiansen said. "But most of them who stay at the cemetery stay because that's where their body is. They don't know anybody, so they have nowhere else to go."

20

Attacks in the Dark

Something uninvited resides in the house where eighteen-year-old Michelle and her family have lived for twelve years. She knows it is a spirit. It touches her. "Before I go to sleep I can feel it," Michelle said. "I look at my closet and I can tell when it's going to happen."

Michelle's room sits over the furnace and is warm in the winter, unless the unseen thing is there. "When I don't feel the spirit, it's all white walls and it's warm. It feels warm," she said. "Whenever it's there, it feels cold, sharp, and distant. It always comes from my closet, but I can't see it." She has discovered that, if she feels the presence early enough, noise will keep the spirit at bay. "I turn on my radio. It doesn't come when there's sound on," she said. "If it's silent I feel it will come right before I go to sleep."

This is when it attacks. "I can't move anything," she said. "But my muscles [flex] because I'm fighting. The whole bed will be shaking because I'm fighting it, and then it's gone and I'm exhausted. I pass out." The attacks are known as Old Hag Syndrome because some people who experience them report seeing an angry old woman sitting on their chest during the attack. Michelle's attacks began early in her childhood, and a few years ago were occurring as often as twice a week. Psychologists refer to these experiences as "sleep paralysis," but Michelle said she isn't suffering from a psychological manifestation—she knows the attacks are real. "I used to think it's a dream," she said. "But it's not."

Although the spirit has not attacked anyone else in the house— or attacked Michelle anywhere other than in her room—an ominous feeling often follows her through certain parts of the house: her room, the back of the living room, the kitchen, and the space directly below in the basement. "My sister and I, neither [of us] like the basement," Michelle said. "She can't go in the basement by herself. I feel creepy when I go to the basement too, but I sing really loud when I go down there. I don't know what it is—it's like [there's] somebody else. We have trouble going to sleep at night." Michelle and her sister Stephanie sometimes hear the faucets in the bathroom turn on and off, and Stephanie has seen something in the yard. "Stephanie knows there's something," Michelle said. "There's flowers at the front of our house and she saw a little boy playing with flowers. Then he was gone."

But inside the house, Michelle's mother is the only person who has seen anything strange—and she doesn't talk about it. "Mom knows there's something," Michelle said. "Everybody was in the front part of the house. She looked down the hall and all of a sudden she saw a tall dark man go from our bathroom to her room. She was sure it was Dad, but when she said his name, he called from the other side of the house. 'I think I saw a ghost,' she said." Michelle thinks the figure her mother saw might be the thing that attacks her in her bedroom, but the attacks have disappeared since she has gone to college. However, she is worried about a younger sister, Danielle, who now lives in her room. "It's creepy," she confided. "My room is not natural."

21

It Fell from the Sky

Gray geese dot the water in Big Lake Park as a breeze sends ripples across the water's surface. The yells of children running at a nearby playground echo across the water, while a couple of cars sit pointed at the lake—workers taking their lunch break. Train tracks run nearby, but for now they lie silent. But Big Lake Park, at the northern end of Council Bluffs, was not always so peaceful. On December 17, 1977, something unexpected crashed into the park's frozen ground.

A slight wind blew across the lake that Saturday evening as people traveled across northwestern Council Bluffs—some to a nearby mall, some to see family, others just cruising the night. A dusting of snow coated the frozen ground. It was cold—thirty-two degrees—but not nearly as cold as Iowa can be in mid-December. The glow from the street and business lights of Council Bluffs, as well as those from Omaha, Nebraska, just across the Missouri River, painted the night sky a peaceful slate grey. Mike Moore of Council Bluffs was twenty-four in 1977 when he and his then-wife drove through Big Lake Park at 7:45 p.m. and saw something strange in the sky. "I lived in Carter Lake at the time and I was on my way over to see my mom," he said. "As we were passing Eppley Airfield, we saw this big ball of red stuff in the sky." Initially, Moore thought the light was from an airplane landing or taking off from Eppley, but if it was an airplane, something was wrong. "I thought if it was a red light on a jet, it would have crashed," Moore said. "All I saw was this ball coming down. It was pretty high in the sky when I saw it. I just saw a big ball of flame."

Moore wasn't alone. Three (or four, depending on the report) teens driving to the Richard Gordman store on North Sixteenth Street saw something, too. They "noticed a reddish object about five to six hundred feet in the air falling straight down," according to an article in the Historical Society of Pottawattamie County's December 2007 newsletter. The youths stopped alongside Kenny and Carol Drake and their twelve-year-old nephew, Randy James, and asked if they had seen the object. They had. Mike Moore's father, Assistant Fire Chief Jack Moore, responded to the scene fifteen minutes after the incident and spoke with the Drakes, who told him they had seen "something red" in the sky, according to a December 18, 1977, article in *The Daily Nonpareil*, the Council Bluffs newspaper.

But the "something red" Mike Moore, the Drakes, and the teens had seen wasn't the only view of the object. Moore's ex-wife saw something different than the ball of red light. "She seems to think she saw something with revolving white light going around," Moore said. "Back then, she made the comment [that] she saw something up in the sky with lights orbiting around it. I didn't see anything because I was driving the car." Moore's ex-wife told computer programmer-turned UFO investigator Dr. Jacques Vallee that she saw "a big round thing in the sky below the tree tops. It was hovering. It wasn't moving." Vallee investigated the case for his 1998 article "Physical Analyses in Ten Cases of Unexplained Aerial Objects with Material Samples" for the *Journal of Scientific Exploration*. Moore's ex-wife wasn't alone. Two unrelated people told Vallee they had seen an object with the same revolving white light at 7:45 p.m. that night.

Although the sighting slightly differs between witnesses, one element remains constant—the light in the sky left something behind. Mike Moore saw it fall. "I just happened to be looking that way. I just happen to see this thing coming down," he said. "It was a pretty good sized ball of fire coming down out of the sky." A middle-aged couple who wouldn't give Vallee their names said they had seen the same thing: "a bright red object rocket to the ground near Big Lake." The Drakes told Moore they had seen "something red fall out of the sky to the southeast, hit the ground, and explode into flames."

The Council Bluffs fire and police departments arrived at the scene in less than fifteen minutes, among them Assistant Fire Chief Jack Moore, who told *The Daily Nonpareil* that he found a four by six feet "mass of molten metal" on a levee that night. "It was running,

In December 1977, eyewitnesses reported 1,000 pounds of molten metal falling from a light in the sky over Big Lake Park in Council Bluffs, Iowa.

boiling down the edge of the levee," Moore reported. "The center of it was way too hot to touch." Mike Moore arrived at the scene at 8:15 p.m. and saw the object. "I got there a half hour after it hit and it was still molten. It left maybe a six- to eight-inch crater in the ground as it hit," he said. "I got in there because of my dad. They had it blocked off." Mike Moore described the metal as "a big ball of burning iron," the center so hot it looked like blue flash bulbs. "There was a flash thing in this molten iron that was even melted." The fire department put out fires in the surrounding grass, waited for the metal to cool, and then loaded the material in a truck and took it back to the station. "The fire department picked up a couple of pieces, they left and I kind of hung around and picked up a few pieces that were left," Mike Moore said. "I still have boxes of it in my shed. I've got torches. All the torch did was heat it up. A grinder won't cut it. You can't even bend them." Mike Moore's words echoed those of his father from more than thirty years ago. "I have the pieces in my office," Jack Moore told *The Daily Nonpareil*. "You can't break it and you can't bend it. I know it's metal, period. It's got me beat."

So what was this mystery metal that fell out of the sky?

Investigators ruled out space debris, a meteor, and something dropped from an airplane, leaving one terrestrial cause for the debris—an explanation many agreed with—it was a hoax. But was it? There were two foundries in Council Bluffs capable of producing molten metal and both had immediate access to the Chicago & North Western and the Illinois Central railroad tracks that ran next to the park. However, actually getting that much molten metal onto the levee presents other problems. "To take that much molten iron in a truck, you'd have to have it at two thousand degrees, and it was a heavily traveled road," Moore said. "They were saying there was about a thousand pounds of molten iron laying on the ground. That doesn't explain how four or five people saw it fall out of the sky."

Samples of the metal were taken to nearby Griffin Pipe Products Company and to the Ames Laboratory at Iowa State University. "I recall the examination," said Dr. Francis Laabs of the Ames Laboratory. Laabs did the initial testing and was less than enthused by the results. "We found the debris we received to examine to be consistent with smelter slag, very similar to that from a few operations in eastern Nebraska where they were using auto scrap to make manhole covers, etc. We suspected a hoax." The university found the metal consisted mostly of iron with less than one percent each of chromium and nickel. A portion of the metal was also sent to the U.S. Air Force's Foreign Technology Division at Wright-Patterson Air Force Base for analysis, but the Air Force did not reply to a Freedom of Information Act Request for results of the analysis.

Greg Hoskins of Omaha is a longtime UFO enthusiast and visited the site shortly after the incident. "It was colder than a son of a gun when we got over there two days later," Hoskins said. "The stuff was splattered all over." Hoskins retrieved small pieces of the metal that were still on the ground; the bottoms of the pieces were flat because it was molten when it hit the ground, he explained. "There [were] still small amounts of it," he said. "I had a coffee can of it for years. I gave the pieces of it away. I think I still have the coffee can." Hoskins had the pieces tested by a laboratory, but their findings were the same as Ames Laboratory and Griffin Pipe Products Company— the metal was slag. "I had physical material, but it's not worth anything," Hoskins said. "It was just common. You can get slag from anywhere."

But who could have gotten their hands on that much slag and transferred it to the park in a molten state? Griffin Pipe Products told Vallee that not only would the metal have to be kept at 2,500 degrees Fahrenheit, but the foundry didn't pour on Saturdays, so it could not have been the source of the metal. The great improbability that jokesters could pull off such a stunt has left many, including local UFO researcher John Buder, convinced the incident was not a hoax. "A UFO was several blocks south of the park and was observed by a lot of people on the ground," Buder said. "It moved toward the park, [and] it jettisoned a large amount of metal." It's the people, Buder said, that make the story believable. "The people involved in seeing it in the air had no reason to fabricate this story," he stated. "They were common people driving in Council Bluffs. From two different locations it was observed. They watched it coming in." Another aspect lending credence to the case has been noted by both Buder and Vallee. The incident in Council Bluffs was just one of many similar occurrences around the world in which molten metal was ejected by a UFO. "What it seems to be [is] one of thirteen cases of metal being jettisoned worldwide up to that point," Buder pointed out. "This is the same slag that's been jettisoned all over the world. It was not an abnormal thing for it to be jettisoned." Vallee cited cases in Brazil, Washington state, Washington DC, Sweden, Ohio, Alaska, Columbia, Mexico, and Nevada that were all similar to the one in Council Bluffs—and in all cases, the material was slag. "That's what it is. It's smelter's slag," Buder said. "When I show it to people, they're very disappointed. Maybe they've taken everything out of there that's worth taking and thrown it back at us."

But Hoskins doesn't think the slag came from just anywhere, he is convinced it came from a UFO. "There [were] enough witnesses [that the possibility of] a hoax was taken away by the number of people who said they saw something come out of the sky," he explained. "If [hoaxers] ran up the road and threw it out of a can, they would have [needed] an awful heavy arm."

Buder thinks the nearby railroad tracks have something to

do with the metal hitting the ground in the park. "There have been a number of sightings along those tracks from Council Bluffs to Sioux City," Buder said. He is convinced that UFOs follow the tracks, possibly for navigation. "America was covered with railroad tracks at one time, so it was not uncommon for UFOs to be seen around tracks," Buder continued, reciting a line from a railroad worker song written in 1850. "T'was a dark night, '49, and we was layin' steel, / when we saw a flying engine without no wings or wheels."

But Laabs and others at Ames Laboratory have tried to stay as far away from the UFO angle as possible. "As scientists, we do not editorialize about our findings, but rather make the best measurements we can and infer what our rational interpretations are," Laabs said. "But very rarely will we tell you to believe this or that without sufficient proof. We have no desire to stir up a lot of controversy by publicizing what we think or surmise; rather we reported only the experimental 'facts' as we personally knew them. We measured the material. It was consistent with foundry slag."

Mike Moore doesn't care what scientists say the material is—he knows what he and others saw more than thirty years ago. "My uncle was stopped at a stop sign and lights came up behind him and took off in the sky. He was a police officer," said Moore. He is convinced the light in the sky was something from outside our world. "I think there's stuff out there."

22

Joslyn Castle

The thirty-five-room house built from thick blocks of silverdale limestone sits in what was once the outskirts of Omaha. This spot was once connected to the downtown area by trolley; now it's almost downtown itself. The tall city buildings and new state-of-the-art Qwest Center are visible from this mansion known as Joslyn Castle. Newspaperman George Joslyn and his wife, Sarah, hired architect John McDonald to design and build this house on five-and-a-half acres of farmland; the house cost $250,000 and was constructed in eleven months between 1902 and 1903. The Scottish Baronial structure stands at 3902 Davenport Street among smaller, but still impressive homes, looking like it should be perched by a loch in the Scottish Highlands rather than in a midwestern town founded on the cattle trade.

Because of its location on the outskirts of the city, Joslyn called his property a farm, according to Judy Alderman, education and tour coordinator for Joslyn Castle. "It was right on the edge of town. This was like the last outpost before you went into complete farms. George got into a fight because [Omaha] wanted to make it a part of the city. To prove his point, he bought cows and chickens and let them loose on the lawn." He won his fight with the city, but his victory, as well as his time in the house, was short. George died in 1916. Sarah Joslyn continued to live in the house until her death in 1940; she left the house in the care of a trust to be used for the benefit of the Omaha community. The building was added to the National Register of Historic Places in August 1972, during the time it housed offices for the Omana Public Schools. In 1989, the state took over ownership of the castle, and extensive renovation and restoration work began.

Visitors and employees alike have reported the sounds of invisible parties and the apparition of a young woman in the thirty-five-room Joslyn Castle in Omaha, Nebraska.

Although George and his family made many contributions to the community, including Omaha's Joslyn Art Museum, they left one legacy that will last as long as their home stands—many people believe the castle is haunted.

Nano Little, executive director of Joslyn Castle since 2006, is a little hesitant to say the castle has permanent guests, although she may have met them. "I've heard voices," she said, and she is not the only one. "The people who have heard this will say you hear them in the area of the morning room. You hear them in the right time of day. You can't understand what they're saying. It sounds like they're lilting."

"There're multiple voices," Alderman reported. "But you can't hear what they're saying."

The elevator, installed while the Omaha Public Schools' headquarters were located in the castle, moves to the third floor for no apparent reason and locks there. Thermostats change while employees are out of the building, doors fly open, people walk through unexplained cold spots, and occasionally something touches someone who is in the castle alone—like Joslyn Castle event coordinator Marnie LeGloanec. "I was standing at the front door one afternoon all by myself and I felt someone tug at the back of my hair," she said. "No one was there." LeGloanec also heard something unexplained in the castle in fall 2008. "I heard noises coming from the kitchen," she said. "Pots and pans banging around. It just sounded like a person banging around, so it didn't scare me." Until she realized she was alone. "Then I was a little scared." Visitors to the castle have also claimed to hear dishes rattle in the kitchen pantry. But are people who work there afraid of Joslyn Castle?

"I haven't been afraid," Alderman said. "Just worried."

To keep from getting spooked, Little tries not to think about ghosts. But that doesn't always work. "Sometimes we've waited for people to come before we go over there," she said.

LeGloanec smiled. "I got chased by a bat," she said. "Does that count?"

But not all encounters have frightened people. "A woman heard in the morning room a woman say, 'We're very happy here,'" Little said. "This is a happy place. There are a lot of joyful occasions." The joyous occasions the castle hosts are parties, a Scotch tasting (to pay homage to the building's Scottish architecture), corporate events, and weddings. But these events aren't off limits to the castle's denizens. "There was a bride that got married a year and a half ago [2007] and pictures she was in had orbs in it," Alderman said. "But only pictures with her in them." A year later the newlyweds attended a party at the castle and a picture taken of the bride was marred by a large, white orb next to her face. That was the only picture an orb appeared in that night.

An ornate 1,800-pound cast-iron door protects the front entrance to the castle. A carriage house of similar construction to the castle sits to the right of the front of the castle steps, and the offices of the Joslyn Castle Trust reside in an old outbuilding behind the castle. The 19,360-square-foot castle includes a library, drawing room, plant conservatory, third-floor ballroom, reception hall, and a music room added in 1906. "George wanted it," Alderman said. "Sarah didn't." A tornado destroyed most of the outbuildings in 1913, and a hailstorm pounded the area, damaging many trees on the property in 2008. The castle wasn't scratched.

Two people died in the castle, both of natural causes: George and Sarah. "He actually died in the master bedroom," Alderman said. "Sarah died in 1940. After she died she left the house to a trust. She didn't want any other family to ever live here. We think they're both still around."

Seven different types of wood were used in the castle, and each room was given its own style, from Gothic to French to English. Many rooms are undergoing restoration; the Gold Room has been completely restored to its appearance when the Joslyns lived there. An original tiled vestibule welcomes visitors to the castle. During the day, certain rooms on the ground floor are well-lighted by sunlight that streams through the large, original windows—such as the morning room that Sarah Joslyn claimed as her office, and the conservatory where a padded bench gives a comfortable view of fountains and plants. Sometimes at night, even after everyone has gone home, the castle is still well-lighted. "The lights," Alderman said. "There've been numerous times I've been the last person in here and I've turned off the lights, and I turn around and the lights are on."

The lights have been inexplicably turning on for a long, long time. Jo Grebenick worked at the castle for fourteen years and she got frustrated dealing with the lights coming on after she'd turned them off. "There were a lot of things that happened during the time I would consider paranormal," Grebenick said. "I never really questioned it or truly believed it, but just accept[ed] it. These things happen. And a lot of things you'd expect would happen in the wee hours of the night." Grebenick's office was in Sarah's bedroom on the second floor. "I would leave at night and, of course, turn out the lights," she said. "I was having a problem. I'd leave and go down the stairs and the lights would go on in the office. I'd go up and turn them off and I'd call the state to have an electrician come over." Some of the electric wiring in the building was original, she realized, and might be prone to short, but most of the wiring was relatively new, installed by the Omaha Public School District. "I didn't think it was that, but I wanted to check," she said. The electricians never found a problem with the wiring and the mysterious problem with the lights continued. "One night I was frustrated," Grebenick said. "I said, 'Goddamn it Sarah, I've been here all

The ghost of George and Sarah Joslyn's adopted daughter, Violet, has been reported walking up the stairs of the castle.

day. Just let me go home one night without the lights being on.' I turned off the lights and went downstairs. And they didn't go on and they never went back on the rest of the time I was there."

Grebenick has also heard music on the third floor. "One of the weirdest things that happened, one night I left and I got down to the bottom of the stairs, I heard music and glasses clinking and a muted conversation," she said. "I thought, 'Oh, God, what's that?' I knew I was the only one in the building." At the time, college-aged volunteers would occasionally work in the castle and Grebenick thought one of them might have left a radio on. "I got halfway up that main grand stairway and it stopped. I thought, 'Okay, I don't know if I want to go up there.'" She did, and nothing was on. "I left, and didn't think I'd say anything." She didn't, until a few weeks later when two workmen arrived for the restoration project. "The guys there were having to take off the wall covering one layer at a time," Grebenick said. "They like to start at six in the morning and work until the real good light stops." So Grebenick gave them a key. The next day the workmen were in her office. "They were over at my office early the next morning wanting to talk to me," she said. "They were up on the scaffolding and heard music and like something was going on. One turned to the other and asked if they wanted to go investigate that. And he said, 'Not unless you go with me.'" The two men got halfway up the stairs and stopped; the noise was too much for them and they left for the day. "That scared them," Grebenick said. "I laughed."

But Grebenick didn't laugh at Christine, a director at the nearby Nebraska Arts Council, who came to the castle to discuss her wedding and saw something that terrified her. Grebenick said, "I was with another client upstairs [who was booking the castle for her daughter's wedding], so when [Christine] came, I said, 'Why don't you just sit downstairs for a second. It won't be very long.'" Christine sat at a window seat that looks into the conservatory, and Grebenick went back upstairs to meet the other client. "All of a sudden I hear a bloodcurdling yell [from downstairs]. The mother of the bride had this horrible look on her face like, 'Jesus Christ, what kind of place is this?'" Grebenick ran to the staircase and leaned over. "I said, 'What happened?' Christine was just white. She said, 'I was just sitting there and all of a sudden this woman in white was walking up the stairs. She had kind of a white dress on.'" Christine described the apparition as young, pretty, and wearing "old fashioned" clothing. A week later Christine came back to talk with Grebenick about her wedding and was stunned by a large photograph hanging in the castle. The photograph, donated that week by the Friends of Joslyn Castle, was of the Joslyns' adopted daughter, Violet. "She was in her engagement dress, sitting where Christine was sitting," Grebenick said. "Chris looked at this picture and said, 'Oh my God, that's her. That's the person I saw going up the stairs. Do you think she lives here? Do you think she'll be at my wedding?'" Maybe she was or maybe she wasn't—it would be hard to tell. Violet died decades ago.

Violet, however, hasn't been the only permanent resident seen at the castle. Fred Myers, a former groundskeeper at Joslyn Castle, has seen doors slam for no apparent reason, has responded to clanging alarms when no one was in the building, and has heard the music. "I don't get excited too easy," Myers said. "I'm a little bit hard of hearing and I wanted to hear the music Jo had heard. I'd go in there at night and go to the third floor and wait. The hair sometimes would raise on the back of my neck." He was working in the yard one day when a man hired to work on the windows approached him. "He asks if the castle was haunted," Myers said. "He was working on the windows on the third floor—he's on the outside. He said, 'I'd seen a man walking back and forth on the third floor with a top hat, jacket, and striped pants.' He was right spooked about it. He wouldn't go inside. He said he'd seen it a couple of times. The guy would just walk around, top hat, tails, cane. I always said you had to be crazy to work there after three months, but it was a fun job."

Although Grebenick never saw anything strange in the castle, she never felt alone there. "There were just so many times you felt like somebody was there," she said. "I never saw any visions like that, but other people reported seeing something, or just something in the window, a curtain move, or some kind of figure. But who knows? I never was afraid there. I never felt there was an evil presence. Just probably some of the people who probably lived there. It wasn't demons or scary things."

Apart from private events, the castle is open to the public for tours the first and third Sundays of the month and Alderman said there is always someone in a tour who asks about ghosts. "I think a lot of tours assume it's old, so it has to be haunted," LeGloanec said. Little sees the question as an introduction to praise the castle. "When people ask me, I say, 'If you had a house like this, would you leave?'"

23

The Crying House

Christie Geier-Pratt grew up in Kansas City, spending her youth in one of the grand old houses in the northeast section of the city. The home's large second floor, like many in the neighborhood, had been turned into apartments for soldiers returning from World War II. Geier-Pratt's family moved into the first floor in 1964, just before she began third grade, and left during her sophomore year in high school. During that time, Geier-Pratt's parents returned the upstairs to family living ... and awakened something that would haunt Geier-Pratt for years.

Her father and brothers were running errands and Geier-Pratt was home with her mother and older sister. "My sister was upstairs and my mom was in the dining room," Geier-Pratt said. "She told us to stop crying. We weren't crying." Geier-Pratt's mother called the girls into the dining room, where the sound of a weeping girl spread through the room. "When you stepped into the dining room you could hear this sobbing and moaning," Geier-Pratt said. "It came in waves. It would get louder then it would fade away. If you weren't paying attention to it you would miss it." The crying lasted about forty minutes, but they only heard it in the dining room. The crying didn't make Geier-Pratt uneasy—but the feeling of being watched did. "Never before or never since I lived in that house did I have that feeling of being watched," she said. "It was acute and was frightening at times. It was in my room on the second floor and in a few other parts of the house—it was overwhelming."

So much so that she wouldn't go upstairs at night without her sister and she never changed clothes in her room. "There was a huge stairway that went upstairs and I would wait on my sister who was five years older than me," she said. "I would never go in my room and go to sleep by myself." Geier-Pratt's friends didn't want to stay the night because they also felt they were being watched. "It was just creepy to be in that room," she said. Things would bang in the attic, doors and the downstairs cabinets would slam in the night, and Geier-Pratt felt unseen hands holding hers. "I remember thinking, 'I wonder what it would be like living in a house that wasn't haunted?'" she said.

One night when Geier-Pratt's older sister, then a high school senior, came home from a date, they both experienced something that made them tell their mother they wanted to move. "My sister was dating then and would come back and smoke [on the deck]," Geier-Pratt said. "[One night] she said, 'Stay up and I'll bring you something.'" Geier-Pratt tried to stay awake, but finally fell asleep on her bed. "All of a sudden my bed started going back and forth," she said. "It was like someone was pulling my mattress back and forth. I had to hold on." Geier-Pratt's sister had come home after curfew and, afraid the noise from Geier-Pratt's room would wake up their parents, ran into the room. "I heard my sister running through the room and she jumped on the bed and said, 'What are you doing? You'll wake up Mom and Dad.'" She thought Geier-Pratt had been jumping on the bed … she wasn't. But it wasn't what Geier-Pratt's sister heard that upset her; it's what she saw. "She said, 'You weren't supposed to go on the deck without me and I saw you there,'" Geier-Pratt said. "It wasn't me. [From outside] my sister saw someone get up from my bed and walk out the door." They ran from the room, but something followed them. "All of a sudden I felt tingling from my shoulders to my knees," Geier-Pratt remembered. "I said, 'Do you feel that?' She said, 'The tingling?' Then she said, 'I'm not living here anymore.' Now I had validation."

Geier-Pratt's family moved from the house in 1972. "Lots of people have different experiences growing up, and they are just what they are," Geier-Pratt said. "But when we moved I had peace, peace to live."

24

The Hotel Savoy

The Hotel Savoy rises for seven stories above the Kansas City pavement. It is an elegant living tribute to the glory days of this historic cow town, when jazz musicians wailed in smoky, gin-soaked clubs and mobsters conducted business behind the backs of the police. When the owners of the Arbuckle Coffee Company built the red brick hotel in 1888, the Savoy boasted a ballroom, carved woodwork, marble walls, and a rooftop garden. The building, which was placed on the National Register of Historic Places in 1974, fell into disrepair by the 1960s and has been undergoing restoration ever since. According to the hotel website, many famous people have stayed at the hotel, including celebrities Will Rogers and W. C. Fields, Presidents Theodore Roosevelt and William Howard Taft, and business tycoon John D. Rockefeller. The Savoy, described as "a fine European Bed and Breakfast," still welcomes guests visiting Kansas City overnight, or staying for the long term in one of its rooms-turned-apartments. The Savoy Grill restaurant, which opened in 1903, is the oldest restaurant still operating in Kansas City—it has seen Presidents Warren Harding, Harry S. Truman, Gerald Ford, and Ronald Reagan. A prankster once locked Harry Houdini in a telephone booth at the hotel, and the big band tune, "Stompin' at the Savoy," was recorded by Bennie Goodman and Count Basie. Although the rich and famous from the hotel's heyday have long since gone from the Savoy, some of the building's history still roams its halls. According to those who work there, the Hotel Savoy is haunted.

Long-time bus staff, like John Rivera, have heard stories over the years from guests who all report seeing the same thing—someone staring at them from mirrors in their room. "Sometimes they see a face

Something haunts Room 505 of the Savoy Hotel in Kansas City, Missouri—
something that just wants to say "hello."

in the mirror brushing their hair," Rivera said. He has also heard story
upon story about room lights flickering, invisible hands touching guests
in the night (sometimes a welcome massage), phantom carts squeaking
down the halls, a top-hatted shadow walking in the basement, and
the ghost of a little girl who stalks the fourth floor. The one element of
these stories that impresses Rivera is their consistency. "These people
don't know each other and they experience the same phenomenon,"
Rivera reported. Waiter Curtis Hough, who worked at the Hotel Savoy
two different times for a total of about ten years, saw the ghost of the
little girl just off the stairs between the fourth and fifth floors. At first
he didn't know what he had seen. "In 1990, they started the restoration
of the hotel," Hough said. "In the bed and breakfast rooms I thought I
saw a little girl about age ten in a long dress—Victorian style—up on
the fourth floor. I came down and asked anyone if they should get their
kid from upstairs and they said there were no kids on the premises." It
wasn't until Hough discovered the story that he realized what he had
seen. Rivera has not seen the ghost of the little girl, but he has heard
enough to know it's on the fourth floor. "Guests have seen a little girl

with a long flowing dress," Rivera said. "She just stands and stares." Although management doesn't promote these stories, the tales of the haunted hotel persist. The daddy of which is room 505.

Legend has it a woman died in the bathtub of room 505. Visitors have said the shower curtain shuts by itself and the water comes on. The room was turned into an apartment, but the stories of people staying there vary. Mike Dobbins, who in 2004 lived in 505 (one of eight apartments at the hotel), had not had an encounter with the shower specter and doesn't think she exists. "I haven't seen anything," he said. "I haven't heard anything. I had someone who'd come in here and said she'd sensed something, but I'm not in tune with that sort of thing." Many others claim to be.

Rivera said a lot of people—people who want to find the ghosts of the Savoy—have visited the hotel year after year, especially on Halloween. "There's a lot of people who come here," he said. "A lot of weird people." Larry Green, general manager of the hotel, said he doesn't think there's anything to the ghost stories. "I've been here ten years and I've never experienced anything," he reported. "We've had people come in who've heard stories and are disappointed. They were expecting something to happen."

But Anne Bishop of Lee's Summit, Missouri, is a believer. Bishop has stayed in room 505 and she knows it is haunted—she has experienced it herself. "There's more than one ghost in the place," she said of the hotel. Bishop was staying with her brother who lived in room 505 when she encountered some of the spirits of the Savoy. Bishop and her brother had gone to a club for a couple of drinks, and she had come back early and fell asleep on the couch. "And I had a dream that was one of these dreams that was not a dream," she said. "I dreamed I was on the couch sleeping and there was two women and one man standing over me talking about me." Bishop, who said she is sensitive to the spirit world, is convinced this was not a dream, but an encounter. "I know the difference between when I get messages from the other side," she explained. "I know when it's a dream or something in my head. It was very distinct who was standing there."

Bishop, a registered nurse, had attended a medical conference in downtown Kansas City when she stayed with her brother a second time. "He went to spend the night at his girlfriend's house and all of a sudden I just thought, 'I'm going to be in here by myself?'" she said. "I remember standing in his bedroom and saying, 'Listen, I know you're here, but I really have to get up early so please don't jack with me.'" She slept in her brother's bedroom with the lights on, but that didn't stop whatever inhabits 505 from saying hello. "I'm a smoker and never go to bed without my cigarettes and a lighter next to me," she said. "The next morning, the lighter was gone and I thought, 'What the hell?'" She was going about her morning routine, getting ready for work when she walked back into her brother's bedroom and found the lighter. "In front of the bathroom door, from the middle of my left thigh, the lighter just, 'boom,' appeared and slipped down from inside my pants and right out in front of me," she said. "I just said, 'good one.'"

Bishop said things like this happen to everyone all the time; we just don't recognize it as anything abnormal. "The world is a much more magical place than people give it credit for," she said. "It's about our culture. Our minds are just not very open." And she is convinced the Hotel Savoy is one of those magical places. "There is no doubt that there is stuff going on there," she said.

The Hotel Savoy is at the corner of Ninth and Central Streets in downtown Kansas City, Missouri. The telephone number is 816-842-3575; call them and rent a room. Who knows what might find you in the night.

25

The Ford House

The stench of death clung in the air around the entryway closet of Misti McKenzie's rural home. In 1968, McKenzie's parents built the house about a mile east of Richmond, on the spot where the parents of Robert Newton Ford, a hanger-on of the James Gang, once lived. Hoping to collect reward money from the state, Bob Ford planned and carried out the assassination of the outlaw Jesse James at his home in St. Joseph, where he was living under an assumed name. Ford was murdered in Colorado ten years later, and is buried in the Richmond City Cemetery just a few yards from David Whitmer, one of only three people said to have seen the golden plates from which Joseph Smith transcribed the Book of Mormon.

McKenzie's family lived in the Ford house for a short time before tearing it down and building the new house. "Not too long after we moved in [to the new house], there was a terrible smell that came from the entryway coat closet," McKenzie said. "Mom was convinced we had a dead mouse in the wall and tore out drywall in the closet and the basement below in an attempt to find the source." McKenzie's parents never found a source for the smell, but knew it wasn't a natural smell because it never went away. "It was so bad we couldn't store our coats in there," McKenzie said.

Eventually, McKenzie's mother turned to a professional to find where the smell was coming from. Not an exterminator, not a carpenter or a plumber, but a psychic. "Mom always had an interest in spirituality, psychics, and metaphysics," McKenzie said. "She was a pretty darn good psychic herself but she never wanted that to get out too much." During a gathering hosted by McKenzie's mother, two psychics claimed to have discovered the origin of the smell of death. "She met two little old ladies who were ghost-busters" McKenzie said. "They believed that there was the spirit of a Confederate soldier that had run away injured from the battle at Lexington."

McKenzie had doubts about the story. The Battle of Lexington, which took place from September 18 to 20, 1861, was twelve miles away—quite a distance for a wounded man to travel. The soldier would also have had to cross the Missouri River, which wasn't likely. "They said he died there where Mom's house was built," McKenzie said. "They helped his spirit make his crossing to the light—he apparently had great remorse for running away and left unfinished business and I guess that is why he got stuck in our closet."

After the spiritual cleansing, the smell of death was gone. "After nearly fifteen years, we could finally hang coats in there. The smell never returned," McKenzie reported. "To this day, if I think about it, it can feel sorta creepy in that entry hall if I am there alone. My son is living in the house now and does his best to keep that story as far in the back of his mind as he can—understandably so."

McKenzie's son, Ray Smith, said research on the Ford house revealed it wasn't a soldier from the Battle of Lexington who died in the home; it was Bob Ford's brother Charles, who shot himself through the heart. "Charlie Ford committed suicide in the house that was once out there," McKenzie said. "The little old lady ghost-busters thought the young man had died from a head wound and had taken up staying in the closet because he was confused. Could it be that Charlie Ford was hanging around in our closet, trying to find his way home?"

But, as with many places marred with tragedy, Charlie Ford was not the only one to try to commit suicide there. "One more creepy little sideline in this story is that my Mom's Uncle Sammy was one of the last people to live in that old [Ford] house before it was torn down," McKenzie said. "He attempted suicide by shooting himself, but was unsuccessful. Obviously, Uncle Sammy was never quite the same again. I don't remember much about him except he scared me as a little girl. I do remember seeing blood on the wall of the upstairs bedroom."

McKenzie also remembers bullet holes in the walls of the old Ford house and a trap door in the floor. "I was told the trap door led to a tunnel that came out down the hill from the house and was used as an escape tunnel," she said. But like the original house, the Ford family, the blood on the wall, and the smell of death, "any evidence of that is gone."

26

Ufos and Cowtown, USA

UFOs don't appear only in remote areas over the heads of solitary individuals; they also appear over urban areas over the heads of thousands of potential witnesses—many of whom simply don't look up. The Mutual UFO Network (MUFON)—an international group that investigates unidentified flying objects—receives dozens of reports of UFO sightings in the Kansas City area each year. Many of the cases are simply unexplained lights, such as those seen by a motorist named Garrett who was driving from Olathe, Kansas, to Kansas City, Missouri, at about 9:30 p.m. in August 2007 when he saw three or four "strange lights" hovering. "These lights were in a crescent moon shape and were disappearing randomly, then appearing again in another area of the sky," Garrett said. "They were also moving in ways that a normal aircraft could not." The lights moved side-to-side, in zigzags, and in circles. "Did anyone else see these things?" he wondered. Mostly likely they did not, or they simply didn't report them.

Other reports are of an unidentified craft and, on rare occasions, a case will include contact or telepathic communication. "I was about four-and-a-half years old. I was sitting on the front steps to my house," Fred of Kansas City wrote in his MUFON report. "I saw, suddenly from the east, a UFO come into view. ... I kept mentally asking for a ride. I suddenly got a reply, 'No. Not now. Not yet.' Being a kid, I got angry and shot three rolls of single-shot caps at it. A few minutes later, it flew back east." This was in 1950.

Most reports do not include contact. Jim Johnson, director of the Kansas City chapter of MUFON, said the group's objective is to apply scientific methods to the investigation of UFOs. But simply seeing a strange light or reporting mental contact is not enough to attract the attention of MUFON. The group needs physical proof, or at least corroboration, in order to make the investigation worthwhile. "It's hardly credible if only one person saw it," he said. But one-person reports make up the majority of UFO sightings, so the Kansas City area only has "one or two" UFO cases a year MUFON considers worthy of an investigation.

But those who see strange lights in the sky believe differently.

Police Sighting

Gary Buchanan was a Kansas City police officer in 1960. He and his partner, Richard Dawton, were working the "dog watch" from midnight to 8:00 a.m. one Saturday when they saw something strange in the sky. "About 2:00 a.m., we drove to St. John and Hardesty and were sitting at the northeast corner of Budd Park," Buchanan said. While they were filling out reports, a bright light appeared and hovered above their car. "There was no engine noise at all," he said. Just as suddenly as the light appeared, it shot away into the western sky from a dead stop to gone in the count of three. "Dick and I just sat there and stared at each other, and then I said, 'Should we put this in our log report?' His response was, 'Well, I guess that depends on how much you like psychiatrists.'"

They had seen a UFO. And, no, they didn't report it.

A UFO in Broad Daylight

A 1997 event in Kansas City that Johnson investigated himself happened in broad daylight. This type of sighting—a singular witness over a busy area—is all too common. "Many of the reports I have received over the last decade and a half with MUFON are from high-traffic areas," Johnson said. "I was able to get to one of the scenes within an hour or so of the sighting event." The witness of this event, Johnson said, was convincing. "Whatever she saw, she wasn't making it up," Johnson stated. "[She] took me back to the location where she turned off at Southwest Trafficway at Thirty-fourth Street [another busy intersection], traveling north."

The oblong object—shaped roughly like a rugby ball—moved slowly over a television tower, then toward a second television tower about a mile away before it "blinked out." "It lasted a couple minutes," Johnson said. "Her impression was that others were seeing it as well, as cars were slowing down and pulling to the right lane, but she was the only one who stopped." Like the other UFO sighting, there were no news reports about it the next day. So why is it no one else reported seeing these UFOs moving slowly over busy streets in the middle of the day? "I have come to believe that in many cases, the people who are supposed to see flying objects, see them repeatedly, and the rest of us see them rarely, if at all," Johnson said. "Keep in mind that most people aren't looking for them and don't want to get involved even if they do see them. The rest of us keep looking up."

Kansas City, Roswell, and an Eight-year-old Boy

The e-mail message was cryptic. "Hello. I might have some information you will want to hear." No further explanation—just a telephone number. "Any hints?" I pounded across the keyboard. Three hours later, a second e-mail waited in my inbox. "What? Sorry. I thought you wanted information. UFO. No reply is necessary." The man sent his telephone number again, and his name. At his request, I'll refer to him as Marty. I called and Marty answered the telephone. His voice, which once sang with a Navy choir, was scratchy and weak. Doctors had removed half of a lung from cancer and damaged his vocal chords while removing a lump from his thyroid. Marty is sixty-seven years old. But he didn't want to talk about himself—he wanted to share something he had kept hidden for fifty-nine years.

Marty was eight years old in 1949 when his father took him to the Pickwick Hotel at the corner of Tenth and McGee Streets in downtown Kansas City, Missouri. The hotel sat next to a Trailways Bus Company station; they were meeting a high school friend of his father who was stopping there on his way through town. Marty doesn't remember the name of the man who walked into the hotel and greeted Marty's father, but he remembers he was in uniform. "This man was in the service," he said. "I can't tell you what branch."

The three went to a room in the hotel and, as the adults sat at a table and talked, Marty sat on the bed and tried to entertain himself. After a while, he started paying attention to the conversation, and the men noticed. "They said, 'Whatever you hear, stop remembering,'" he said. Then Marty heard things—classified things.

The man had worked at White Sands Missile Range in New Mexico—site of the atomic bomb test. He said whenever the military tested a new missile there, unidentified flying objects would appear to observe the launches. "He said when they shot a missile up to test it, this thing would come up to it and fly around it," Marty said. "These things would come up, circle it, and—*swish*—go away." Then Marty's father asked a question and his friend's voice dropped to just above a whisper. But Marty heard everything. "Pretty soon my dad said, 'I heard a rumor about Roswell and a [UFO] crash,'" Marty recalled. "My dad's friend got real serious and he said, 'I can't talk about that.' But he said it did happen and it was real. This man talking to my dad positively confirmed what crashed in Roswell was true and legitimate."

Soon after, Marty and his father went home and didn't discuss that night for months. "After that, my dad—six months later—said, 'I want you to come with me tonight,'" he said. Marty's father took him to a UFO meeting in Kansas City. "Those people were as squirrelly as squirrels," Marty said. "My dad just sat there and chuckled. He said, 'What you saw tonight was horse hockey. You know the truth and we can't talk about it.' And he never mentioned it again. He wanted me to know the truth and what isn't the truth."

Marty's father died at fifty-one years old in 1961 and neither he nor Marty ever mentioned the strange conversation in the Pickwick Hotel. "This happened years and years ago and I was sworn to secrecy," Marty said. "I've never talked about it."

Until now.

27

1859 Jail, Marshal's Home and Museum

Independence, Missouri   89.10 miles from home

Green shutters frame the windows of the red brick building: the 1859 Jail, Marshal's Home and Museum. The building, just off the historic Independence Square, once housed the marshal and his family in the friendly upstairs portion of the building. But downstairs, the cold limestone cells housed criminals, Southern sympathizers, and, for a time, Frank James. The marshal's home is decorated with period furniture and seems welcoming enough, but the cells are unnerving— many tour guides have said they never feel alone there. "You feel like you're being watched," said Lindsey Gaston, former development director at the Jackson County Historical Society. And for good reason. "If you're sitting in the front, it's not uncommon to hear the [cell] doors open and close. There's some obvious sounds of metal hitting stone. Unfortunately, you get kind of used to it."

People have reported human-shaped shadows moving through the marshal's home and jail, someone staring out of a top window at night, and the unexplainable smell of bread baking in the rear of the museum. But the most curious anomaly associated with the home, jail, and museum is the smoke. The building is on the National Register of Historic Places and is owned by the government, so smoking is prohibited. Still, the unmistakable scent of cigars is often in the air. "About the second day I was over there in the back jailers' stairs, there was the very heavy aroma of cigar smoke," Gaston said. "I thought it was just me, and I mentioned it to someone and they gave me this smile and said, 'Yeah, that happens all the time.'" Tour guide John Cianciolo, who has volunteered at the jail since 1989, said the smoke is real. "The smoke's in different rooms, but mostly in the sheriff's office," Cianciolo explained. "They tell me Frank James smoked cigars. It may be him."

If the ghost is Frank, he may have become awfully fond of Cianciolo. In the summer of 2006, on the way home from flying radio-controlled airplanes with a few friends, Cianciolo realized he wasn't alone in his truck. "I was thinking it was such a fantastic day I'd do it again tomorrow," he said. "As I was thinking what plane I would take out, all of a sudden in my truck I smelled cigar smoke. I looked at my passenger side and just for a second I saw a silhouette shaking its head no. It dawned on me I had two tours scheduled the next day so I couldn't go."

But according to records—although those from the Civil War are a bit sketchy—no one has ever died in the building. Some paranormal experts, like the late Joyce Morgan, a member of the Missouri-based Miller's Paranormal Research group, say most spirits aren't bound to the place where they died—they can come and go, just like the living. Morgan had investigated the James Farm and was convinced the James boys visited there, but never stayed. The smoker could be the marshal, a prisoner, or Frank James.

Frank was never really a prisoner in the jail. He was more of a guest. Frank turned himself in and lived in a nicely furnished cell his jailers kept unlocked. He would have supper with the marshal's family and enjoyed visitors. Frank's cell is kept much as it was when he was a guest at the jail, and the people who work there think Frank doesn't like change. The morning after a Christmas tree had been put in Frank James's cell, tour guides coming in for the first shift found it outside the cell. Although Cianciolo was once hesitant to admit that something—maybe even Frank James—haunts the marshal's home and museum, he is not anymore. "He's never scared me," Cianciolo said of the entity. "He just lets you know he's here." Sometimes with a practical joke.

Cianciolo arrived at the jail early to conduct a special tour one day in March 2007. He was the first one there. The day was cold and the building's thermostat was set at fifty-two degrees. Cianciolo went to the museum in the back of the building and turned the thermostat dial only to watch in surprise as the dial turned itself back down. "I set it up to seventy and it turned back to fifty-two degrees," he said. "It did this two or three times." Then, from across the room, the door leading to the second floor flew open. "When the door came open I went to close it," Cianciolo said, and as he did, the furnace roared to life. Apparently, whoever haunts the house has a sense of humor. "When I walked back over it was at seventy degrees, and I swear I heard somebody laughing."

28

The Schirmer UFO Encounter

Bright blue flags hang from streetlamps that run along Ashland's main drag; some are decorated with yellow flowers, others proclaim "Welcome." Behind the flags, awnings shade brick storefronts that house a bank, an ice cream parlor, and the office of the local newspaper, *The Ashland Gazette*. Ashland sprang up in the mid-1800s when settlers from Kentucky and other eastern states made their way west. Even the town's name is from Kentucky—an admirer of statesman Henry Clay named the city after Clay's hometown of Ashland, Kentucky. The first business in Ashland—Fuller and Moe's General Store—opened in 1863.

Today, the town (population 2,550) sits off the interstate that connects the two biggest cities in Nebraska, Omaha and Lincoln. Being close enough to commute to either one, but far enough away from both, makes the streets in Ashland quiet. But, like in every small town, things aren't always as simple as they seem. On December 3, 1967, a relatively new police officer in Ashland, Herbert Schirmer, saw something on a dark stretch of highway at about 2:30 a.m. that made his life hell.

From The Ashland Gazette, December 7, 1967

"UFO SIGHTING" BRINGS
PUBLICITY FOR ASHLAND

Ashland Police Officer Herb Schirmer revealed Tuesday he had seen a 'UFO' in the south part of Ashland near Highway 6 in the wee hours Sunday and the *Omaha World-Herald* broke the story in its Tuesday evening edition.

Mr. Schirmer was alone in the police car about 2:30 a.m. Sunday, driving southwest on U.S. 6 approaching the 'Y' where State 63 joins No. 6. The highways were deserted, and the policeman says he saw a lighted object over the slope, not far beyond the point where motorists turn off on No. 6 to come into town. He continued to the little loop of road that encircles a tree on the right side of the road beyond the junction and turned around to see what was there.

"As soon as my headlights, which were on bright, struck the object," he said, "I knew it was no truck, and what I saw scared me." Afterward he drew a picture of the type now familiar in UFO stories, of an elliptical object about the size of a room "perhaps 20 feet long and as much as 14 feet thick" surrounded by lighted portholes, connected by a line or a band which might have been paint and might have been some sort of catwalk, he said.

'Flashing lights'
When the police car's lights fell upon the object, the inner cabin lights of the unidentified flying object began to flash off and on, Police Officer Schirmer continued. The craft was hovering just a few feet off the ground, partly over the highway and partly over the shoulder next to the ditch and the rather steep embankment. It was absolutely soundless, Mr. Schirmer went on, and the glow that could be seen at the bottom must have been some sort of ray rather than any sort of jet propulsion device, he speculated.

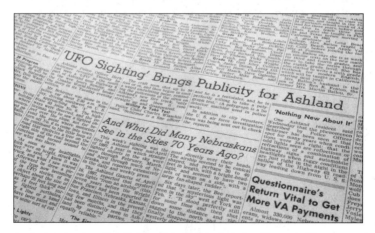

On December 3, 1967, Ashland, Nebraska Police Officer Herbert Schirmer encountered something he said was from another world.

The craft soon shot up to 50 feet or so, and then began to emit a weird undulating noise, reminding the policeman of the siren on Ashland's new fire truck, "only weirder," and then it rose straight up and disappeared.

Willing to take a test

Police Chief Charles [sic] Wlaschin said, "Schirmer is a fine officer and he is a teetotaler, and he is perfectly willing to take a polygraph test." (A polygraph is a lie detector machine used in police work).

In addition to city reporters, the U.S. Air Force investigation team was being sent out to check the reports.

A sidebar to the story quoted an unidentified Ashland resident as saying the lights Schirmer described were "nothing new," claiming the phenomenon described by Schirmer has been seen at that spot for years and attributed them to car headlights reflecting off highway signs. A second sidebar quotes *Gazette* readers saying Schirmer's account was not the first time a UFO had been seen in Ashland. Residents had been witnesses to the great airship wave of 1897:

> Mrs. Cornelius and son, while returning home from church [through dark streets, as Ashland had no streetlights then] about 9:00 o'clock that preceding Sunday evening, saw something "quite small ... about the size of an ordinary room. It appeared not far from the ground and was hovering over the western part of town. Its flight was rapid and it moved toward the north. Twice it flashed its brilliant lights and shortly passed beyond the range of vision."

What did Schirmer see just off the highway in Ashland in the early hours of December 3, 1967? UFO buffs, paranormal researchers, and the United States government have debated the validity of Schirmer's story for more than forty years.

Herbert Schirmer

Herbert Schirmer was, as he described himself in decades-old interviews, "a service brat." He was born in Missouri and hopscotched the globe with his mother and five siblings to destinations like Japan, Germany, France, and Hawaii as his father was transferred from base to

Officer Herbert Schirmer said he encountered a UFO at this spot on Highway 6 on the outskirts of Ashland, Nebraska.

base. John Buder of Bellevue, Nebraska, a retired Air Force chief master sergeant, may know more about Schirmer than anyone. Buder, the assistant state director for the Nebraska chapter of the Mutual UFO Network, has researched him for the past five years. "First of all, he was not a good old Midwest boy by any stretch of the imagination," Buder said. "He'd been raised all over the world." Local ties, as any small-town midwesterner knows, are a vital part of their identity. If your family has only lived in the community for one generation, you're still an outsider.

Schirmer never graduated from high school and enlisted in the Navy at seventeen; he was first stationed at Jacksonville, Florida, and later served a tour of duty in Vietnam. One reason Schirmer may have left high school early, Buder speculates, was because of his twin brother: "Schirmer didn't do too well in school. His problem was that his twin brother excelled and he fell behind." However, while Schirmer was serving his country (as all his siblings would eventually do), there was an accident. "He had a severe head injury in the Navy," Buder said—a detail that would be discussed when authorities investigated the events of December 3.

When Schirmer left the Navy, he moved to St. Louis and got married. Penniless and jobless, he and his new wife moved in with

Schirmer's parents in a trailer park in Memphis, Nebraska, five and a half miles from Ashland. The elder Schirmers ran a bait shop and Herb's father worked a second job for the county. But the younger Schirmer needed work and he set his eyes on law enforcement. "Schirmer wanted to go on the state highway patrol," Buder said. "He'd gotten his GED, which would have qualified him." The only thing Schirmer needed to apply was a statement from a police department that he had never been convicted of a crime. The closest police department was in Ashland, and when Schirmer went to the police station in July 1967, he had a pleasant surprise. "While he was getting [the statement]," Buder said, "the police chief hired him on the spot."

With a new city, a new job, and a new career, Schirmer took to law enforcement with the zest of a young man on a first date. He rousted high school kids drinking beer on city streets and shooed off young couples at a local lover's lane atop a hill at the eastern edge of town. "Schirmer had a reputation of being a hotdog," Buder said. "But he was a good policeman. He took his job very, very seriously."

December 3, 1967
The early Sunday morning was quiet as Officer Schirmer made his rounds on the outskirts of Ashland. At about 1:00 a.m., Schirmer began to feel uneasy, like something was wrong. He patrolled alleys and the local sale barn before heading out to Highway 6 to check on the two gas stations on that lonely stretch of road. He stopped at the stations at 2:20 a.m. to see if anything was amiss, such as jimmied doors or suspicious cars. "He stopped at every business and shook the doors," Buder said. "He was a good cop."

Schirmer radioed the Sheriff's Department at nearby Wahoo, Nebraska, at 2:30 a.m. and told them everything was secure, then he pulled onto the highway and encountered something that would haunt him the rest of his life. "He went to the end where he usually turned around and saw what he thought was an overturned truck," Buder explained. He stopped his patrol car about fifty yards from the lights. "I felt nothing at first, then tingly," Schirmer would later say. Instead of an overturned truck, Schirmer saw a silver, shining oblong craft hovering a few feet off the ground. He hit the high beams and

when the intense light struck the craft, it brightened. As the patrolman slowly pulled his vehicle closer to the object, it started to rise
and emit a pulsating wail. A "flame-colored glow" flared from the
underside of the craft, and it shot straight up and disappeared into the
night. Schirmer stepped out of his patrol car to investigate the area
and discovered nothing unusual. After the five-minute drive back to
the station, Schirmer speculated the entire event lasted about ten minutes—but when he pulled into the station, it was 3:00 a.m. He didn't
think about it until later, but the times didn't add up.

At the station Schirmer, visibly shaken, drank coffee and talked
about his encounter. An officer on duty offered this advice: shut up
about it. According to Buder, "[The officer] said, 'Don't tell anyone and
throw away that report. I have seen the little green men outside their
machines driving from here to Wahoo.'" Buder added, "Even though
he had actually seen landed craft with occupants outside, he would
not tell anybody." The officer knew Schirmer would be ridiculed if he
filed a UFO report, but Schirmer wrote in the station's logbook, "Saw
a flying saucer at the junction of Highways 6 and 63. Believe it or
not!" Schirmer, suddenly racked by a searing headache and a strange
buzzing noise in his head, didn't sleep well that night. He later found a
red welt behind his left ear.

What Schirmer didn't realize was that those sixteen words
he wrote in the station logbook would attract the attention of the
national press and the United States government.

The Condon Committee
By February, the Condon Committee, which investigated UFO cases
under the direction of University of Colorado physics professor Dr.
Edward Condon, wanted to know more about the Schirmer case.
On February 13, Schirmer and Police Chief Wlaschin arrived in
Boulder, Colorado, so experts could hear Schirmer's story, analyze
his psychological makeup, and figure out just what had happened on
December 3. Schirmer's testimony was designated case 42. Dr. Leo
Sprinkle, an associate professor of psychology at the University of
Wyoming, was the first person to interview Schirmer under hypnosis
and had a positive impression. "He was an interesting fellow and he

was willing to talk about his experience," Sprinkle recalled. "There were a couple of things strange from his standpoint. He viewed himself a good policeman from the sense of duty, and he saw himself having a psychic sense that he knew when something was strange." Using the pendulum technique to put Schirmer under hypnosis, Sprinkle talked the police officer back to December 3. What he found was things Schirmer himself had not remembered—events that had never been spoken of began dropping slowly into the conversation. "He said he reached for his pistol when he saw the thing [UFO] and he reached for the microphone, but he didn't follow through with it," Sprinkle said, mentioning Schirmer thought he was under someone else's mental control after he saw the UFO. "He felt that, yes, he was in contact with someone during the encounter. There was a definite feeling he was given information."

In an interview soon after the event, Schirmer said that legs descended from the craft as it landed. Something unseen and unheard (directions from the alien presence, Schirmer later decided) prevented him from removing his firearm from its holster and from radioing about the sighting. After the craft touched down, a hatch opened and lights poured from the spaceship. A human-like figure appeared to walk from within that light. Another being left the craft and approached Schirmer holding some device that it pressed against Schirmer's neck. The figure asked, "Are you the watchman here?" Sprinkle said, and Schirmer agreed. "He was watching as a good policeman would." The entity told the "watchman" to come with it

SCHIRMER TALKS UNDER HYPNOSIS

'Fuzzy Space Man to Visit Me Twice More This Year'

Ashland Policeman Herbert Schirmer said under hypnosis that a white, fuzzy, man-shaped form approached him from an unidentified flying object he says he saw at 2:30 a. m. last Dec. 3

Most of the above stories were not mentioned in any of the officer's recollections in the few days immediately after the alleged incident.

Schirmer underwent hypnosis and revealed more information about his encounter—information that made his personal life an emotional hell.

148

and Schirmer followed it into the first level of the craft, reaching it by floating through the air. Schirmer found them standing in a circular room where the being explained to him that the craft operated by electric and magnetic forces that could control gravity. Schirmer said the entity told him the ship was feeding off nearby power lines, then the being showed Schirmer a second level full of instruments before depositing him back outside the craft.

From The Ashland Gazette, February 22, 1968

SCHIRMER TALKS UNDER HYPNOSIS
'Fuzzy Space Man to Visit Me Twice More This Year'

Ashland Policeman Herbert Schirmer said under hypnosis that a white, fuzzy man-shaped form approached him from an unidentified flying object he says he saw 2:30 a.m. last Dec. 3 near the "Y" intersection of Highways 6 and 63 south of Ashland.

His recollections while hypnotized were reported by Police Chief William Wlaschin after sessions at a meeting with the Unidentified Flying Object Study team of Boulder, Colo., early last week.

Ashland Mayor C.M. Goff confirmed at the City Council meeting at the City Hall Thursday night that he had given permission for the pair—two-thirds of Ashland's full time police force—to make the journey to Boulder together.

Officer Schirmer, as seen on KETV television Friday night, said the white form struck him in the neck.

He told the Boulder investigators that the visitors were not from the solar system but from a neighboring galaxy, "although they have bases on Jupiter and Mars."

He said he was told they and the space craft would make two more visits to him (Schirmer) some time in 1968.

Most of the above stories were not mentioned in the few days immediately after the alleged incident.

Dr. Leo Sprinkle of the University of Wyoming conducted the hypnotic examination at Boulder. He told the *World-Herald* by telephone late last week "that there is no guarantee that recalled information is more reliable than what was previously reported consciously."

The trip to Boulder and the hypnotic session there provided all three major Nebraska dailies with a field day in feature writing. The *Lincoln Star* printed 12 column inches on the story; the *Lincoln Journal* 19 inches; and the *Omaha World-Herald* 13 inches one day and seven the next.

Some Ashland residents are convinced that what Officer Schirmer saw was a type of reflection of lights from nearby sign boards or his own police car headlights when foggy conditions in that low part of the valley are just right.

As soon as the first report of the "sighting" was made in December, city reporters and UFO enthusiasts zeroed in on the young officer who was put on the police force last year.

When Schirmer and Wlaschin returned home, they found at least part of the town enraged by the attention Schirmer had brought upon them (most probably the teens Schirmer busted for beer and partying, Buder speculates). A mannequin with the name "Herb" written across it was found hanged by a noose in a local cemetery and Schirmer started receiving threatening telephone calls. "One of the older people in town said to me [that Schirmer] was a little strange when he arrived," Buder said. "But he became a little stranger when the UFO story came out." But, despite the opinion of the townsfolk, Sprinkle was sure Schirmer was telling the truth about his abduction. "I think it's a good case," Sprinkle said. "The reason I think it's good is because he was a policeman and he was willing to talk about his experiences. He thought it was true." Although Sprinkle felt Schirmer's testimony was convincing, other members of the Condon Committee weren't sold. Their report read:

Condon Committee Case 42 conclusion: Evaluation of the psychological assessment tests, the lack of any evidence, and interviews with the patrolman, left project staff with no confidence that the trooper's reported UFO experience was physically real.

Schirmer's Life Gets More Complicated
Months after Schirmer's UFO experience, his headaches and the strange buzzing noise remained. He would wake up and find himself

choking or handcuffing his wife, and strange dreams gave him fitful sleep. The behavior of some Ashland citizens didn't help. "Herb had a rough go from people around him," Sprinkle said. "Not only affecting his job but affecting his marriage as well." During this time, he was approached to write a book about his experience.

From The Ashland Gazette, April 4, 1968

SCHIRMER AGREES TO WRITE UFO BOOK

Channel 7 newscast news Saturday evening showed a picture of Ashland policeman Herb Schirmer signing what was said to be a contract for a book he is to write telling of his experience late last year when he said he saw an unidentified flying object, was talked to by a space man, and was hit in the neck by the latter, near the Highway 63-6 "Y" south of Ashland.

The newscast said Patrolman Schirmer was to receive 40% of the profits of the book.

Then Schirmer's life seemed to jump into overdrive—he was promoted to the top level of the police department.

From The Ashland Gazette, April 18, 1968

SCHIRMER ELEVATED TO CHIEF OF POLICE

Ashland Police Chief Bill Wlaschin resigned last week from the Ashland police force and was succeeded by appointment of Mayor C. M. Goff by Policeman Herb Schirmer.

The appointment of Police and Fire Department heads for the ensuing year will be one of the duties of Mayor-elect Paul Lombard at the annual reorganizational meeting of the City Council, scheduled for Tuesday night, April 30.

But the promotion would be short lived; Schirmer resigned from the post two months later because he felt distractions from the events of December 3 and the constant headaches kept him from doing his job effectively. In Buder's research report, "Police Officer Goes Aboard a UFO Craft in Nebraska USA," Schirmer was quoted: "I resigned because I was simply not paying attention to my job … You can't be a good policeman if you have personal problems. So I quit." But he wasn't finished with the night of December 3, 1967. After a local businessman suggested he contact UFO researcher and author Warren Smith, Schirmer called Smith who, with fellow UFO researcher and author Brad Steiger and hypnotist Loring G. Williams, agreed to meet Schirmer to find out exactly what had happened to him.

Schirmer Goes under Hypnosis Again
Under the orange roof of a Howard Johnson in Council Bluffs, just over the Missouri River from Omaha, Schirmer met with Smith, Steiger, and Williams on June 8, 1968, for Schirmer's second interview under hypnosis. "That was a long time ago," Steiger said. "I got involved with the case because Loring Williams was visiting me. We'd do experiments in hypnosis, out-of-mind traveling, the same type of thing." Smith asked Steiger and Williams, "Could you guys come down and interview [Schirmer] and perhaps Bill could hypnotize him?" Steiger, who had written his first book on UFOs, *Strangers from the Skies*, in 1966, was in, and so was Williams. The three met with Schirmer in the hotel and, exercising a healthy dose of caution, made sure they were quiet about it. "We kept [the name of the hotel] really hush-hush," Steiger said. "[Parties interested] might be the CIA or the Air Force or the Men in Black. We didn't want anyone to find out." At the onset, Steiger was impressed with Schirmer's sincerity. "Some of my best friends are cops," Steiger said. "He reminded me of a typical cop. He was very serious." But, at least superficially, Schirmer appeared a bit frightened, or, as Steiger put it, "a little bit in awe of what had happened. He was not a UFO groupie. He knew next to nothing about the subject." Although, Steiger said, Schirmer couldn't have been completely ignorant on the subject of UFOs because they had been the subject of various news reports since the late 1940s. More recently, Steiger had been part of the well-publicized World UFO Conference at the Commodore Hotel in New York in 1966. "Condon was [at the conference]," Steiger said. "Everyone even peripherally interested met in the Commodore Hotel. In 1966, that made all the papers. Then it just faded away. Herb couldn't say that he hadn't heard about [UFOs]."

Under hypnosis, Schirmer told Smith, Steiger, and Williams

that he'd seen a human-like entity wearing a uniform with a feathered serpent insignia. "He said the entity came out and communicated with him," Steiger said. "The thing that both troubled me and intrigued me, [Schirmer] said every once in a while, 'They would talk with me through my mind.' He sounded like a contactee." The trio asked Schirmer under hypnosis what he meant and "he would keep saying, 'They're talking to me in my head,'" Steiger said. "He kept repeating that." In a hypnotic trance, Schirmer talked about the feathered serpent logo and drew a picture of an entity wearing an earpiece with "almost reptilian eyes," Steiger said. "And the patch on the uniform [was] of Quetzalcoatl [the Aztec creator god]. That's what I would call it."

Schirmer claimed the alien entities were able to control his report of the sighting. "I did exactly as they told me, so I was like one of those robots you hear about," Schirmer said, according to Buder's report. "Something also prevented me from giving out all the details when Dr. Sprinkle had me under hypnosis before the Condon Committee. I am certain that these people could control a man through his brain for as long as they wanted." The visitors were "not dumb," he explained and could "zap" the world if they wanted to. The entity told Schirmer "there will be many more contacts with our people. Most of our people will not remember talking with them unless they want them to remember." Although Schirmer reported this, he said he wasn't convinced the entities were telling him the truth. "This might be something to throw us off guard," he said.

Steiger considered Schirmer intelligent and credible, but after the trio interviewed Schirmer that day and the next, everyone went home and Steiger lost track of Schirmer. "What happened after that, I don't know if he went on the circuit and started channeling Bumpha from Mars."

New Evidence
The people of Ashland were quickly ready to be rid of the UFO story. Most people, especially today, don't remember it. "They don't and that's the way Ashland seemed to have wanted it," Buder said. "The kids growing up in Ashland, not one of them had heard of the Schirmer case." After retiring from the Douglas County (Nebraska) Sheriff's

Department, Buder decided to dig into a subject that has fascinated him for a long time—UFOs. "I never doubted their existence," Buder said. "I've never seen a UFO, but I've been able to collect the largest [UFO] library in the Midwest." Because of the proximity of his home to Offutt Air Force Base and to Ashland, the Schirmer case became an easy obsession. Buder interviewed everyone he could find, including friends of Schirmer's, relatives, coworkers, and casual acquaintances. What he found was a body of evidence that proved to him that Herbert Schirmer had encountered an extraterrestrial craft that cold night of December 3, 1967. Some of that evidence began on December 4.

Schirmer and Chief Wlaschin investigated the site of Schirmer's encounter the next day. They found little, save for a "small, thin piece of what they called 'molten metal' that was the same color as the UFO," according to Buder's report. No evidence of a landing, no scorch marks—nothing. Later Geiger counter readings showed a slightly higher radiation level at the site than from the surrounding area, but the State Radiological Laboratory dismissed the readings. Buder said evidence collected at the site where Schirmer said he saw the craft is irrelevant. According to Buder, during Schirmer's missing twenty minutes, he was actually on a nearby hill. "I have the photographs that have the impression in the ground that something had landed there," Buder said. "Close to lines they drew the electricity from." An electric line pole that is no longer there held a scorch mark where, Buder said, the ship "pulled the electricity from the pole."

There's also the water. Buder said water was an integral part of the UFO's reason for landing. "This was an ideal place," he said. A water pipe still stands near the place Buder said the craft landed; it was also the local lover's lane Schirmer had been patrolling since he had joined the police force. But Schirmer knew nothing of the craft drawing energy from water and electricity until his trip to Colorado. "It was only later when he had gone to Colorado and was put under by Leo Sprinkle that he knew this," Buder said.

Although Buder is convinced the Schirmer case is legitimate, there have been moments when he had doubts. "There were periods of time during this investigation that I questioned if it actually had occurred," he said. But then he found other witnesses. Two women who had been driving near where Schirmer saw the UFO reported seeing something similar, as did a nurse's aide in a rest home in Ashland. She was looking out the window on the morning of December 3 when she saw a strange light jet into the sky. On December 31 or January 1, a man was driving near the railroad tracks that run through Ashland, about fifteen miles from where the Schirmer encounter occurred, when he saw an object similar to the one Schirmer saw land on the railroad tracks. Then there was Schirmer himself, who confessed everything to his mother. "I've tried to punch holes in it and the fact that he didn't lie to his mother and told her things he didn't tell anyone else ... she believed her son and I would go along with that," Buder said. Schirmer told his mother the aliens said they were going to visit other members of his family. And maybe they did. "Sure as hell, a few years later she's driving from Ashland to Memphis and she enters a cloudbank and there's missing time," Buder said. "Peter [Herb's younger brother] had a similar incident on the same stretch of road as his mother." Another brother "disappeared from the face of the earth," Buder said. "He's never been heard from. It just adds more confusion to the case."

The effects of Schirmer's head injury in the Navy were investigated during the case, but, as Buder explained, the head injury made more sense to confirm Schirmer's abduction than to discredit it. "Leo [Sprinkle] had led me to believe that [extraterrestrials] ... are interested in what head injuries do to humans. Leo also indicated this is common among abductees and contactees—the head injury."

Whatever entered Herbert Schirmer's life in that cold, clear night in 1967, be it aliens, hallucinations, or psychological trauma, one thing is certain—he never welcomed it and he never enjoyed it. "It destroyed his life," Buder said. "He's been shattered by it. It's caused him nothing but misery from that point on. He's never gotten [another] police job. Now he's a subcontractor putting on roofs. It's really hurt him." Schirmer doesn't talk about his encounter anymore, Buder said. He has had enough.

29

Near-Death Experiences

Chris Brethwaite of Raytown realized there was something more to life than just being alive when he was in high school in the early 1970s. Brethwaite walked into his kitchen late one night—he had just returned home from his job at a local pizza parlor in his hometown of Phoenix—and ate a bowl of cereal. When he finished, he set the bowl on the kitchen table and his view of the universe changed forever. "I saw and I heard that cereal bowl move about four inches across the table," he said. "I was dumbfounded by the experience." He mentioned the incident to his father a few days later and was shocked at his father's response. "He had a coworker who had dropped dead of a massive heart attack that week," Brethwaite said. "My dad had seen his friend in the doorway of his bedroom. I believe the two experiences were related. I believe it was that man's soul who moved that cereal bowl and he chose to make his presence known in a non-threatening manner."

These incidents convinced Brethwaite that human consciousness continues after death. A few years later, in 1976, his father died and gave him further proof of this. "Several months after he died, my sister woke up in her apartment and was convinced she saw my dad standing at the end of her bed," he said. "Then she left the lights on in her apartment the next few nights."

After that, Brethwaite picked up a copy of Dr. Raymond Moody's 1975 book, *Life after Life: The Investigation of a Phenomenon–Survival of Bodily Death* and began his search for answers to his questions on life after death. "There's more to life than what we realize," he said. "In 1975, Moody came out with his book and I have followed the literature trail ever since."

Brethwaite's mother died from cancer in 2006 and has helped

fuel his search. "We've had things happen that we're convinced it was my mom communicating with us," he said. In November 2007, Brethwaite's sister called him at work (Brethwaite is a humor writer for Hallmark Cards in Kansas City, Missouri), which was unusual for her. "My sister never calls me at work," he said. "She was getting ready for work that morning and opened a compartment on her dresser to take out a piece of jewelry that belonged to Mom, and all of a sudden she smelled Mom's perfume." As soon as she smelled the perfume, the picture on the television in her bedroom went gray. Her first thought was the cable went out, but she could still hear the television on in the living room. She couldn't think of anything in her room that would have a scent of her mother's perfume and, if it did, why she hadn't smelled it before that day. And she couldn't figure out why the picture on the TV screen went down. "She was baffled by this experience," Brethwaite said. "One of the things she couldn't figure out was the significance of the date." Brethwaite telephoned their brother in Phoenix and asked if that day meant anything to him. It did. His brother and sister-in-law had just come back from court, where they had received legal custody of the Brethwaites' younger brother who has Down syndrome. "That was the last piece of business that was unfinished from Mom," Brethwaite said—but his mother has made her presence known in other ways. "My sister and I have had experiences where we've smelled votive candles in the house when we have no reason to. We assign that to Mom who was a devout Catholic. Not only have we had these unexplained experiences, but these unexplained experiences have been on very significant days."

Such an experience occurred with a clock in Brethwaite's home. "The only habit my mom had was collecting clocks," he said. "I only have one clock similar to what she would have collected. At the one-month anniversary of her passing, it stopped at the time of her death. If there is no life after death, you would not have ghost stories or psychic dreams and visions—I don't think those things would exist."

Because of the paranormal occurrences in his life, today Brethwaite helps people who have had similar experiences. "It's one thing to read about a near-death experience in a book or a magazine," he said. "But when you sit down with an experiencer and they share their experience firsthand, you can hear the sincerity in their voice. You can see the emotion of the experience in their eyes." In mid-2000, Brethwaite contacted the International Association for Near-Death Studies, a support organization for people who've had a near-death experience, and offered to start a local chapter. "They have chapters in most major cities," Brethwaite said. "They didn't have a chapter here in KC, so a couple of years ago I asked about starting a chapter and they were interested." The international group has been around since the early 1980s and not only offers "experiencer" support, but provides information on near-death experiences to the public and researches incidents of near-death experience. Near-death experience is a term coined by Moody in his 1975 book to describe what happens when a person dies and is brought back to life, but reports that while dead they communicated with deceased relatives or angelic beings.

Ken Prather of the International Association for Near-Death Studies shared his own near-death experience with Brethwaite at the group's 2007 leadership conference in St. Louis. "Ten years ago he was walking home from work and a carload of guys leaped out and beat him—I'm sure killed him—with baseball bats," Brethwaite said. "He was in a coma." While Ken was unconscious, he saw and communicated with angelic entities. "One minute he saw a baseball bat coming at his head and the next minute he was talking to celestial beings," Brethwaite said. "He had a very profound near-death experience." Ken has mobility issues as a result of the attack, but doesn't regret what happened to him. "When I was talking to him, he said they'd never found the five guys who did this," Brethwaite said. "He said if he'd ever see them on the streets one day, 'I would buy them a beer. What happened to me was such an incredible experience that what they did to me was a small price to pay for it.'"

Brethwaite believes Ken because he has heard the same results from so many people who have had a near-death experience. "These people are changed. They become more loving, caring, altruistic, non-judgmental. Sometimes their spouse thinks someone else came back," Brethwaite said. "If it was just the brain manufacturing stuff, they would be able to put it in human language. There are not words to adequately use to express what they experience." Brethwaite said that each person who has had this experience is adamant it was real. "The experience was more real than this world. These people have lost their fear of death. I think for that to happen, it has to be a profound experience. If all of us were 100 percent convinced there was something beyond this lifetime, I think we would get more joy out of life."

One other piece of evidence that leads Brethwaite to believe in after-death continuation is deathbed visitations. Many dying people will report seeing a dead relative or friend in the room with them, but the person appears as they did decades ago, not like they looked upon death. "Some deathbed-type visions are probably from a dying brain," he said. "But I believe that some people on their deathbeds do in fact see deceased loved ones or some type of angelic type entity … when someone goes through an NDE [near-death experience], it takes them a moment to recognize the deceased loved one. … if this was all hallucinatory, I don't think your brain would make them look like they did decades ago."

The Kansas City chapter for the International Association for Near-Death Studies meets the third Sunday of every other month at the Unity Temple on the Plaza in Kansas City. The meetings are free and open to the public, but there is a love offering for the church. "Me or somebody else will talk for the first hour on one given topic," Brethwaite said. "And for the second hour we talk about what anybody wants to talk about. Usually people will share paranormal experience with the rest of the group." These experiences range from after-death communication to deathbed visions, ghosts, and reincarnation. "Any topic that has any connection with life after death," Brethwaite said, "we explore."

30

Haunted
by Helpful Spirits

Micaela Daley's family moved to an older, two-story home in Seward in 1991 when Micaela was five years old. It didn't take the house long to let them know it was watching them.

"My mom was pregnant with my brother, and my sister was fifteen," she said. "My sister had the typical '90s big hair. The thing that was seen, my parents thought it was my sister." Micaela's mother was home on a workday with morning sickness when she saw someone walking to the second floor. "She went upstairs," Micaela said. "She thought it was my sister. Then she remembered Wendy was in school. It was the middle of the day." As Micaela's mother ascended the steps, she heard water dripping. When she got to the bathroom, she noticed that someone hadn't removed the plug from the bathroom sink. "The sink was almost ready to overflow," Micaela said. "My mom was really creeped out."

But the family soon discovered it wasn't just Mom who was seeing things. "Friday and Saturday night my dad likes to stay up and watch movies on TV," Micaela said. "He was sitting in the living room. He thought he heard someone walking around in the kitchen, so he got up. He thought he saw someone who looked like my sister walk through the door."

However, Wendy had already come home for the evening and was asleep in bed. Micaela's father started to look for the figure he had seen, but smelled something burning in the kitchen. "There was a bag of hamburger buns sitting on a burner that had been left on and was about ready to burst into flames," Micaela said. "It was probably my sister. She's kind of careless." After he moved the buns and turned off the burner, Micaela's father looked for someone in the house—but only his family was there.

Whatever was in the house wasn't finished warning the Daleys when something was wrong. "We were all sleeping and my mom has this ridiculously good sense of smell," she said. Her mom smelled something burning. "Dad checked it out. He heard someone in the basement walking down the stairs. He went down there and he saw the furnace had caught fire. We stayed at a hotel that night." The Daleys were never really uneasy with the figure—who looked like Micaela's sister—because it only showed up when something was wrong. "The first couple of things were helpful," Micaela explained. "That all happened within the first year. Nothing happened to me until I was a little older."

When the Daleys moved into the house, they didn't have air conditioning and young Micaela left her door open for the breeze. After air conditioning was installed, she started closing her door at night. "I collected Beanie Babies," she recalled. They were lined up on a shelf mounted high on her wall. "The first night I kept my door closed, I heard the bean sound. *Thump, shunk.*" She tried to ignore the sound of Beanie Babies striking and sliding down her wall and eventually fell asleep. "When I woke up the next morning, there were five Beanie Babies on the floor near my door," she said. "But they were only the ones with wings. That happened three times." Micaela thinks whatever is in her house didn't like her door shut.

Wendy and Micaela oftentimes smelled pipe tobacco in the house, although no one in the house smokes. The Daley family also occasionally saw figures move in their periphery. "All of these things happened between the ages of five to eight," Micaela said. "My dad talked with the family that lived there before and the parents thought the kids were crazy because they [the parents] didn't experience things, but the kids did." Wendy is convinced there are two spirits in the house: the girl her parents have seen and a child that may have thrown Micaela's Beanie Babies. But since something has saved the Daley's house from fire and flood, they're not eager to rid their home of its helping spirits.

31

Something at the Bedroom Door

Early one morning, Alicia Stanley heard a baby cry. Her fiancé, John, had already left for work, her eight-year-old daughter was not yet awake, and the baby … well, Stanley was feeding the baby.

When Stanley and her family moved into the two-story, seventy-year-old house, they were surprised to find the house already had a resident. "I have heard a young child several times and it is usually very early in the morning when I am feeding my son or getting ready for work," she said. "I know that sometimes I hear the child and it sounds like it is coming from my son's room." Or—even more disturbing—she has often heard the child crying out from a passageway that connects the baby's room to the master bedroom, but when she opens the door to the passageway, it is empty.

But the baby's room is home to more than the sound of a crying child. "He has a deck off of his room that has long sliding blinds and it has sounded before that someone [was running] their hands across the blinds to have them clank together," she said. "There is no venting close by that would even cause that."

The noises escalated … then things got physical. While she was downstairs one morning, a loud bang brought Stanley to the staircase. "There was a crash down the stairs and there was a [curtain] rod at the bottom of the stairs," she said. It was a curtain rod from the baby's room. "It sounded like someone had chucked it down the stairs."

And Stanley has seen something in her house. While sitting in the living room, she often sees movement on the stairs. "A lot of times out of the corner of my eye I will see something," she said. "To me it looks black and I am expecting something to come down the stairs—and when I turn to look, there is nothing. There is light all the way up the stairs, so it's something that blocks the light."

During the weekend of April 5, 2008, the activity in Stanley's home escalated to the point of terror. "Over the weekend my fiancé and I were asleep in bed and we both heard someone or something coming up the stairs and our bedroom door knob jiggled," she said. "I sat straight up because it sounded like someone was in our house, about to walk into our bedroom." That night, Stanley said, was the only time she has been afraid of her house. "I was never scared until I heard those footsteps in the dark and the door knob jiggled," she said. "I was okay with it when I was hearing the child, but now at night when I hear the footsteps I don't get the same feeling."

Doors Stanley knows were closed are later found open; lights she knows were turned off are found turned on. Stanley knows she is not the only one experiencing these things. Her fiancé, her daughter, and her two dogs have all reacted to something heard, but not seen. "My fiancé is never home in the mornings because he leaves so early for work, but this Monday he was home with our son and had put our son down for his morning nap, and was very startled when he heard movement upstairs," she said. "When he went up there to check on our son, he didn't see anything out of [the] norm."

Cries in the night, footsteps, a black blob on the stairs, and a jiggled door handle have all made Stanley question her sanity, but not like the morning something spoke to her as she put her son in his car seat. "My daughter is notorious for dragging her feet in the morning, and I was stressing about being late because of that," Stanley said. As she buckled the baby in, her back turned to the open front door of the house, she heard a voice—and it wasn't her daughter's. "I heard what I thought was her holler 'Mom' and it sounded like it was coming from the doorway in the house," Stanley recalled. "I started to holler back because I thought she couldn't find her shoes or coat and I was getting cranky because we were running behind, and I hollered back 'What?'" Stanley was surprised to find her daughter standing next to her, asking whom she was speaking to. Stanley was also surprised to see the front door shut.

"I am still trying to decide if it's my mind playing tricks on me or if I am really hearing and seeing something," she said. "I try debunking things as they happen, but I am running out of explanations."

32

Jim the Wonder Dog

Cheating The Rules ... Just This Once
Why do I say I'm cheating? This story doesn't fit the criteria of the
book—not because the story itself doesn't fit in a book about ghosts,
time travel, UFOs, demon possession, and Bigfoot, but only because it
took place more than one hundred miles away. There are a lot of stories
I didn't include because they fell outside my search parameters, like the
Missouri Monster (or Momo) Bigfoot sightings of 1972 in Louisiana,
Missouri, the time machine inventor in Lyndon, Kansas (it was so, so
close), and giant catfish at Bagnall Dam in south-central Missouri. They
were simply too far away. So what makes this story any different? It's
about a mind-reading dog. I really wanted to include it, so I did.

Jim the Wonder Dog
Chain restaurants and motels, Wal-Mart, and a John Deere dealer drape
the few miles of U.S. 65 that pass through Marshall, along the highway
that connects Albert Lea, Minnesota, with Clayton, Louisiana. Marshall
is a town of about 12,000 in Saline County, and was once the home of
statesman and jurist John Marshall (for whom the town was named),
jazz musician Bob James, and the late Mitch Geisler—former mayor
and a police officer during the investigation of the Clutter murders
described in Truman Capote's *In Cold Blood*. But Marshall's best-
known resident wasn't a lawman, a politician, a soldier, or a musician.
The town's most famous resident was a dog.

The Marshall Chamber of Commerce boasts "Smart dog, nice
folks..." and anyone from Marshall will tell you the same. Marshall
was once home to an English Llewellin setter named Jim the Wonder

Mary Burge of Arrow Rock, Missouri, holds a dress she wore as a small girl in the 1930s when Jim the Wonder Dog—a dog people claimed could read minds—picked her out of a crowd.

Dog—a dog who could read the written word and, according to legend, could read minds. There aren't many people left who remember Jim personally—he was born in the Taylor Kennels in Louisiana in 1925 and died in Marshall in 1937. But Mary Burge remembers Jim. Mary is a resident of the nearby town of Arrow Rock, a town frozen in time—so frozen it was the setting of the 1973 movie musical *Tom Sawyer*. Mary didn't care as much about Tom Sawyer as she did about Jim. Well, Jim and her little red dress.

Standing in the Saline County Historical Society building in downtown Marshall, near the newspaper office, the Saline County Courthouse, and the Red Cross Pharmacy, Mary held the little red and white polka-dotted dress on a hanger. The hanger was an antique and so was the dress—it hadn't fit since the 1930s when Mary was a child and part of one of Jim the Wonder Dog's miracles. She grinned as she talked about Jim, and for good reason. "I had this dress on and a red and white spotted bow," Mary said. Her family had come to town that Saturday to shop and had gathered in Marshall's meeting spot, Sam

VanArsdale's Ruff Hotel (the name not dog-related). "Mr. Sam [Jim's owner] said 'Jim, go to the girl with the red dress on.'" Jim went to a group of girls standing in the hotel lobby—Mary was one of them—looked at each one and walked back to his owner. "There were three of us with red dresses," Mary recalled. "So [VanArsdale] said 'Go over to the girl with the red and white polka dotted dress.' Well, there were two of us. He went back and you could tell he didn't know what to do." Then VanArsdale narrowed it down for Jim. He told him to pick the girl with the polka-dotted bow in her hair. The dog walked to Mary. He'd picked the one girl with a bow. "And [Jim] just gave a sigh to say 'I'm glad I finally found the girl.'"

Unusual? Not for Jim. When VanArsdale got the pup in 1925 from a fellow hunter, he just hoped Jim would be a good quail-hunting dog. Jim was good—exceptional even—and was featured in various rural magazines for the birds he could scare up. But when Jim was three, VanArsdale discovered Jim knew a lot more than a dog should. "To me he was psychic," said Mildred Conner, president of the Saline County Historical Society. "They don't want me to say that, but he knew things before they happened."

During Jim's life, he picked seven straight Kentucky Derby winners and the winner of the 1936 presidential election. He could predict the sex of an unborn baby, and was able to identify different types of trees, shrubs, and cars. He understood commands in English, Spanish, Italian, French, German, shorthand (yes, he could read), and Morse code. VanArsdale could not read the requests to Jim written in a foreign language or shorthand, so he would just show the request to Jim and say, "Do whatever it says." And Jim did. Jim could also pick out license plate numbers, find a visitor from a certain place, or find a man wearing a certain color of clothing. "[VanArsdale] said 'Jim, someone's in here with brown and white shoes,' and Jim went and picked him out," said Ken Yowell, executive director of the Marshall Chamber of Commerce and Jim the Wonder Dog buff.

But Jim could also find things he could not see. On another Saturday, Mary's family had again congregated with others at the Ruff Hotel when VanArsdale, a friend of Mary's family, asked Jim to show off. "I had a new purse," Mary said. "It was red and green and yellow, and I was so proud of that purse, and my dad would give me ten pennies." The ten pennies were for young Mary to spend on her trip into town. "Mr. Sam said 'Jim, go over and get the purse with the ten pennies in it.' And he did. I started crying because that was my money for two weeks [and she didn't want Jim to have it]. He didn't ask color. He asked for the purse with ten pennies."

Scientists and veterinarians at the University of Missouri tested Jim and, although Jim had a wider-than-average brow for a setter, the scientists and veterinarians concluded he was just a normal dog— even though he responded to requests in many foreign languages. "They thought the owner was giving him hand signals," Mary said. "But he didn't do that."

Apart from the wide brow, the only physical attribute people would comment on was Jim's eyes. "They almost hypnotized you," Mary said. "As a child, they looked right inside me. He could talk with his eyes." Yowell can see that in Jim's portrait. "The eyes are not a dog's eyes," he said. "They're human eyes."

Although during Jim's life he was featured in *Field and Stream*, *Missouri Ruralist*, *Missouri Life Magazine*, *Ripley's Believe It or Not*, and *The Kansas City Star*, VanArsdale never exploited his dog for fame or money. "Hollywood came in and offered [VanArsdale] all kinds of money, and he said no way. He wouldn't do it," Conner said. "Mr. VanArsdale didn't want to exploit the dog."

Jim died of natural causes March 18, 1937, and was buried near Marshall's Ridge Park Cemetery. The long, slightly sloping lawn dotted with old trees sits close to a golf course and municipal swimming pool, the splashes and hoots of children occasionally breaking the silence under the great shade trees. Jim's grave rests at the end of a concrete path, marked with a headstone that reads "Jim the Wonder Dog: Mar. 10, 1925–Mar. 18, 1937." Although he was buried beyond the cemetery, the cemetery's boundaries grew and eventually spread to include the grave of Jim the Wonder Dog. Yowell explained, "You couldn't bury dogs in the human cemetery, but they moved the boundaries." Each year, Jim's grave receives many visitors, who have developed the tradition of tossing coins on the headstone.

A group called Friends of Jim dedicated a park and water garden

Visitors travel to Jim's grave to drop coins on his headstone for luck and to see the Jim the Wonder Dog Memorial Park and Garden at the Saline County Historical Society Museum.

to Jim the Wonder Dog on May 1, 1999. The park, at 105–109 North Lafayette—right next to the historical society building—features the history of Jim on signs placed throughout a short walk through the garden around a pond and a statue of the dog. "When I first started here in 2000, you could come up any time of day and there'd be people in the dog garden," Conner said. That day, six people wandered into the park, read about Jim's exploits, and took pictures of each other in front of the statue. Darlene Savage, of Jefferson City, was with the small group. "It really was an amazing story," she said. "Somehow that dog was touched."

The group later went into the Saline County Historical Society museum where magazine articles and newspaper clippings about Jim are displayed behind glass. Visitors can also buy the *Jim the Wonder Dog* VHS tape, the book *Jim the Wonder Dog* by Clarence Dewey Mitchell, Jim the Wonder Dog T-shirts, dog dishes, postcards, and "I'm a Believer" buttons. Additionally, visitors can make a donation to the Jim the Wonder Dog Memorial Park and Garden. Yowell estimated that thousands of people come to Marshall every year just to find out more about Jim. "Some believe. Some don't," Yowell said. "I do."

The Friends of Jim can be contacted at: The Friends of Jim, c/o Court Street Classics, 69 South Lafayette, Marshall, Missouri 65340; by telephone at (660) 886-2260; or by e-mail at cscantiques@socket.net.

There. I hope you liked this story enough to forgive me for cheating.

33

Epilogue
Adventures in Ghost Hunting

There is one basic rule in ghost hunting that takes precedence over all others. It is more important than "Take extra batteries," it completely overshadows "Never go alone," and it thumbs its nose at "Don't trespass." This is Jason's Ghost Hunting Dictum: "You will experience nothing out of the ordinary." Seriously. I don't care how haunted a place is supposed to be, if you go looking for something paranormal to happen, it won't. Ghosts have a sense of humor like that. You cannot make a Black-Eyed Kid show up at your door, you cannot will a UFO to appear over your head, and, and no matter how many times you throw yourself against a brick wall, you are not going to project yourself through a portal into another dimension. But it would be fun to watch somebody try.

Then why do so many paranormal groups find evidence of paranormal activity? Because they want to. Most are equipped with infrared cameras, digital audio recorders, and EMF meters and, yes, they do record anomalous pictures and sounds. But who in the heck said any of this is proof of ghosts? No one with authority. Until science proves the existence of ghosts and tells us how to detect them, EMF spikes, orbs, and strange noises are nothing out of the ordinary. That said, there are many, many paranormal research groups that use the scientific method to try and detect paranormal activity. I respect that, and wish them good luck.

You will, however, experience the paranormal completely by accident. I have seen strange things, but they were all random occurrences and never happened to me again.

But, I still look for them.

As an example of Jason's Ghost Hunting Dictum, below is a ghost-hunting trip to a lonely little cemetery in rural Kansas. What did we find? Absolutely nothing. But it was still fun.

Round Mound Cemetary (it was spelled like that on the sign)
Shades of red and pink stained the sky above Round Mound Cemetery like it had been wiped with raw beef. The cemetery sits in the shade of a small copse of trees atop a hill surrounded by a sea of dead fields. Gravel roads tendril from county-paved highways in this rural area, some that lead from Atchison, Kansas, to the nearby small town of Cummings. Brady Cummings (no relation to the town) of Kansas City, Missouri, first heard of Round Mound Cemetery from friends who lived in the area. Local legend has it that a witch is buried there, although genealogical records are somewhat sketchy on the subject of witches. The legend says the cemetery is haunted—that the wind doesn't blow on top of the hill, and the dead scream from their graves.

In the early fall, when temperatures were still high enough to break a sweat, Brady, video engineer Will Murphy (of NWMSU's Department of Mass Communications), and I planned to travel to the cemetery armed with cameras and recorders to see what would happen. It was now January.

Brady had been to the cemetery as a kid, but we needed GPS to help us find the site. A gravel road dropped from a county highway just after a bridge and snaked between fields, branching off toward the hill. Brady's friend Kurt once had a bad experience at that bridge. "The Round Mound story," Kurt said. "Easily the weirdest, most confounding thing that's ever happened to me."

Kurt had gone to the cemetery one night with five other people, including his friend Brian. They got out of two cars and Kurt, Brian, and another walked ahead; the three girls with them were behind. "As we go up the path, we all see a light moving between the trees," Kurt said. "All of a sudden, when we're about three-fourths of the way up, the light stops and starts running towards us. Another light pops ... on the side

171

Round Mound Cemetary (it's spelled like that on the sign) outside Cummings, Kansas, is said to hold the grave of a witch who howls in the night.

of the path. We turn around and haul it to the cars. As we run, more lights appear on either side of the path." They hopped into the cars and drove to the highway. "I get out of my car," Kurt said. "And go to the one behind me to see what we're doing." The people in the second car yelled at Kurt, telling him to get back in his car. He turned, and lights came from under the bridge. "There are lights just off the side of the road," Kurt said. "We drive down to the intersection east of there, everyone decides to go home. Since I live by Cummings I drive back down past Round Mound. There are still lights moving along the path."

Although Kurt said the most logical explanation is flashlights, he is not convinced the lights were not supernatural. "When the lights moved they moved more smoothly than someone running with it could," he said. "And there didn't appear to be anyone behind the lights." He also saw a light in a tree too small to hold a man's weight. "The lights looked like flashlights the way they were moving around," he said. "But some were in places that would be impossible for a person to be."

Yep. That's what we were looking for: strange lights, witches, a windless hill, and the screaming dead.

Will pulled his car through a wide-open, home-welded gate that sat down the hill from the cemetery and parked on the brown

The lone mound on the plains that gives the cemetery its name. Ghost hunters claim mysterious lights chase visitors from the cemetery grounds.

grass just outside the cemetery grounds. Stone walls blockade Round Mound Cemetery; its entrance is a series of pipe gates built like the queue at an amusement park. We wound our way in and prepared for the night. Will and I brought cameras, Will brought the type of hand-warming packets hunters use, and Brady brought stomach flu.

Soft, rounded gravestones from the 1800s were scattered among sharper granite ones. A few colorful plastic flowers sat at the occasional grave, showing someone still remembered. January in Kansas is cold. Especially when the wind blows across the plains. Especially when you're standing on a hill surrounded by those plains. And especially when you're standing in a haunted cemetery on a hill where the wind isn't supposed to blow. I thanked Will for the hand warmers. We took pictures and, as the sun left and night threw black across the sky, we waited for the dead to howl.

Then we saw lights. Two of them, crawling along the base of the hill. We jogged to the front of the cemetery and looked over the stone wall for a better look. The lights were coming closer, winding up the gravel road toward the cemetery. They stopped.

"Isn't that by the gate?" Will asked.

"Yep," I said.

Will used his keychain remote to flash the headlights of his car as we ran from the cemetery. The lights were from the caretaker's pickup. He had almost locked us in for the night.

Later, as the three of us sat in a restaurant in Atchison, laughing at the fact that: (1) we experienced nothing paranormal, (2) we froze our tails off, (3) we were almost locked in a cemetery, and (4) we had stopped at the one restaurant in town that didn't serve beer, we realized something—we had still had a good time. Oh, except for Brady. He got sick in the restaurant bathroom. Ghosts? Witches? The dead screaming from their graves? Not scary. Throwing up a $15 steak? Yeah, that's pretty horrifying.

Afterword
What I've Learned

This book took about two years to write, and I discovered you cannot research and write a book, drive many hundreds of miles through four states, and interview more people than the FBI without learning a few things. The main thing was that I could actually feel the nearness of the paranormal. It is almost as overwhelming and as thick as Midwest humidity. Knowing that your next-door neighbor had been abducted by a UFO, that your child's teacher plays with a Ouija board, or that the drive-up teller at the bank has dreams of things that will soon happen may be enough to make some people claustrophobic. But they'll just have to deal with that, won't they?

A few of my observations are less unnerving. Others, uh, well ...

1. If you trespass, people will shoot at you.
2. Nothing is as it seems. It is much, much weirder.
3. John Wayne was born eighty-two miles from my house.
4. Ghosts seem to be harmless. Demonic forces are not. Can you tell the difference before the monster is out of its box?
5. One hundred miles is not a great distance, unless you have to drive it in opposite directions the same day.
6. UFOs, ghosts, Bigfoot, and Black-Eyed Kids don't have time schedules, don't pick favorites, and don't have prejudices. You encounter them when you encounter them—you can't make them come out and play.
7. Convenience stores are: (a) anything but convenient, and (b) should never post a sign boasting of both "homemade pizza" and "fishing worms."
8. The paranormal frightens people for a reason. Just like in regular life, if you are in an uncomfortable situation, get out before something eats you.

Of course, this doesn't mean you shouldn't look for things that walk in the periphery of the place we call reality. Heck, it's fun, and I encourage you to do so, as long as you keep it safe. The rules for emulating ghost hunting shows on TV are the same as watching Bugs Bunny cartoons as a kid—don't. It will all end in tears. Even though it doesn't seem that way, TV ghost hunters are working in a controlled environment. You are not. For anyone who plans to investigate the paranormal in their neighborhood, take note of the following.

Remember Jason Offutt's Observation No. 1. If you're going to venture onto private property, get permission from the property owner first. Spending the night in jail for trespassing with guys who are in there for things a tad bit worse probably isn't much fun.

If you are going onto public property, understand that public property is not always public. Cemeteries, city parks, and other such venues have operating hours. Cemeteries and parks are open from dawn until dusk. If a cop catches you there at midnight, you are trespassing (refer to Jason Offutt's Observation No. 1).

Never go anywhere alone. You might need to borrow money for beer on the way home.

Think like a Boy Scout. Take the following, and more: flashlight, compass, matches, camera, audio recorder, binoculars, notebook, pens, extra batteries, a coat, cell phone, knife, food, water, and a GameBoy—it gets boring sometimes. Oh, and a crucifix. You never know when one will come in handy.

You are most probably not going to experience anything paranormal. This doesn't mean nothing paranormal happens there, it probably does—the ghosts just don't like you. I have camped in a Victorian mansion on the spot where the ghost of a former occupant often appears, waited for hours on a lonely gravel road where a spook light bounces through onlooker's cars, and sat in cemeteries until I got really sleepy—and I have seen nothing. I have had my share of unexplained encounters, but I wasn't looking for them at the time (see Jason Offutt's Observation No. 6).

One of the dangers of writing a book like this is the fact that I am going to leave something out. Are there more stories of the paranormal within one hundred miles of my back door than I have included in this book? Of course there are, and readers will let me know. But these stories—interesting *true* stories that will give you the willies and cause you to see Shadow People dancing through your room at night—have been omitted completely by accident. That's where you come in. You have a back door; open it and step outside. You never know what you're going to find.

If you know any paranormal stories I missed, please let me know. I can be reached at jasonoffutt@hotmail.com and/or Jason Offutt, P.O. Box 501, Maryville, MO 64468.

Happy hunting.

About the Author

Jason Offutt worked in the newspaper industry for eighteen years and quickly discovered that covering city council meetings wasn't much fun. But, since 2005 when Jason began teaching journalism at Northwest Missouri State University, he started writing about whatever he darn well pleased. He covers paranormal topics in his weekly newspaper column, From The Shadows (also seen at from-the-shadows.blogspot. com), and has written articles for *Nexus Magazine, Fate Magazine, UFO Digest, Missouri Life Magazine,* and *The X Magazine.* His books on the paranormal, *Haunted Missouri: A Ghostly Guide to the Show-me State's Most Spirited Spots,* and *Darkness Walks: Shadow People Among Us,* are available at amazon.com.

Jason lives in Maryville, Missouri, with his lovely family, goes on the occasional ghost hunt, enjoys drinking beer and watching football, and is sure those who won't at least consider that humans evolved from monkeys simply don't have children.